AF584865

Self-Care for New Mums

Self-Care for New Mums

Ruby Matley

Pan Macmillan Australia

Introduction

Motherhood is the relationship that you develop with your baby, but it is also the ever-evolving relationship you have with yourself.

Motherhood is a time of profound personal growth. It is beautiful, messy and filled with unconditional love. It is an incredible and rewarding experience.

Motherhood in the first day, week, month and year is life-altering. This is a new world, a new role. You, your partner and your baby are on a journey of discovery together. It can and will bring overwhelming love, courage and growth.

Motherhood is yours. Embrace it.

Postpartum wellness is essential for all mums, and this can be a time to form new habits and rituals to take with you on a lifelong journey. A baby relies on their mother so much in those first few months, and it is an incredibly special time of bonding as a parent and as a family.

This profound transition can create an opportunity to reconsider and promote your own wellbeing, just when you may need it most. Because, as a new mother, you need just as much nurturing as your new baby.

Self-care is taking the time to support yourself holistically. This can be in a physical, psychological or social way, depending on the needs of your mind and your body.

Self-care can allow you to take a breather and connect with how you feel and what you need. It may help you to feel more energetic, patient and present. And when life becomes overwhelming and chaotic, as it can be in those early days, self-care gives you the tools and strength to help you through.

Self-care isn't selfish, nor is it a luxury. It is a fundamental component of our health and wellbeing, and it shouldn't be left behind after you have had a baby. You don't need to self-sacrifice. You can have time with your baby *and* time for yourself. Sometimes, self-care may be in small snippets or bursts, but as time passes and your child changes and you evolve as a mother, your self-care regime will adapt too.

When deciding what kind of self-care will be best for you, think about what is important to you, what you love and what makes you feel empowered and recentred.

There is no doubt motherhood is hard. It can challenge us; it can be emotional and often in the midst of sleep deprivation and exhaustion, we can feel fragile, covered in a cloud of fog. What I didn't realise during these first days and weeks was that I was becoming more resilient and stronger than I ever thought was possible.

I hope this book will help you to create your own self-care rituals, to support you in early parenthood and beyond.

Welcome to motherhood and to your self-care guidebook.

Ruby

Matrescence is your own birth as a mother.

The term was created by medical anthropologist Dana Raphael in the 1970s to describe the right of passage in becoming a mother. This begins pre-conception, through pregnancy and to birth, then continues to the postnatal period and beyond.

A set of transitions that encompass the biological, psychological, social and spiritual, your matrescence is an individual, personal process. Some say it's a lifelong learning curve.

Every transition to motherhood is different. Your journey may be influenced by:

- your pregnancy experience
- your birth experience
- past traumas or birth trauma
- postpartum healing
- your baby's health and wellbeing
- the physical changes to your body
- learning how to feed your baby, in whatever form that may take.

Each transition should be treasured and honoured.

Becoming a mother

When you become a mother, you experience change on all levels – physical, mental and emotional, and social. It is okay to mourn the loss of your 'old life'.

It's normal to miss those child-free days. It takes time to get into the swing of things with a baby. It's not just a new routine but a new way of thinking, even of being.

Acknowledge and embrace these emotions and allow yourself to miss those experiences. You may find your partner or friends feel the same way. Being honest and reaching out to others can help you to feel less alone during this time of transition.

Growth and change can sometimes feel uncomfortable but know that you will find yourself again. Accepting your feelings may also encourage you to think about new ways of recreating your missed experiences, with or without your new baby.

Ways to constructively mourn your old life include:

- **talking to your partner, friends or family**
- **writing your feelings down, without guilt or self-criticism**
- **engaging in some activities that you enjoyed pre-baby**
- **finding a professional to help you work through any grief.**

Becoming a parent is magical but it can be a challenging transition. You might be asking yourself: Will I enjoy a full night's sleep again? Will I go out for dinner with my friends like we used to? Will I ever be able to exercise more often? I remember thinking these things too. The answer is yes. But it does take time.

You may feel more vulnerable or fragile as you adapt to this immense change. And this is when self-care can be your go-to tool. It will give you little bursts of energy and joy from doing the things you love, and also help to guide and support you through more challenging times when everything feels all too much. Often we don't prioritise self-care and only utilise it when we are burnt-out or feeling overwhelmed. Remember: prevention is better than cure!

I remember looking at other mums with more than one child and thinking, *How do they do it? How do they make it look so easy?* But I soon learnt that we are all facing our own challenges, whether it is related to our baby's physical health, feeding concerns, sleeping and settling, developmental leaps, or our own guilt or grief. We each have a story to tell. Self-care can play an important role in guiding us through these difficult times.

When we become parents, our ideologies and beliefs change as we all come to realise that parenthood is fluid – and things don't always go to plan. We change and grow, and we make decisions based on what feels most right for our baby and our family. Self-care can allow you to focus your attention and be present in the moment. It can help you learn to trust your instincts, and give you the permission to change your mind and grow with the people and environment around you.

It takes time to adjust to the role of parenting and mothering. For some, it is instinctive and comes more naturally. For others, it is a process and takes a little longer. Both are absolutely okay. And it changes again over time, with each child that you have. We are each on our own journey.

Aim to make your self-care consistent and intentional, and allow it to be the support beams for your wellbeing and health.

My journey

During my first year of motherhood, finding even small moments of self-care felt impossible. I didn't have a 'village' to help me fill up my cup after those long days and sleepless nights.

Once my second child came along, I realised that to be the best mother, partner, daughter and friend I wanted to be, I needed to make some changes. This included making time to nurture myself and do the things that I enjoyed.

I knew that research shows that a mother's wellness and emotional health can correlate with and affect the baby's wellbeing. If I didn't feel I could prioritise self-care for my own sake, I had to do it for my child.

Nothing was more important than my health and my family, so I set out to find a way to reclaim those little things that had dissipated from my life. It was like rediscovering who I was all over again. As I got better at making the time for self-care, even if it was just 15 minutes a day, I soon felt less guilty and far more resilient.

Part of my self-care journey included redefining success in motherhood, and finding a way to let go of the unrealistic expectations I had placed on myself, and the guilt that came with inevitable failure.

I realised that the more I practised my role as a mother, the more I grew, and the stronger I became. These past five years have been the hardest, most transformative years of my life – and my best yet.

Yes, I am a mum. But I am also so much more.

Your self-care journey

It is undoubtedly challenging to make time for self-care when you become a parent. You may feel the pull of wanting to be present for your baby 24/7, but you also need space to unwind, recharge and do things that you enjoy.

It can take time to build your confidence as a mother and to find your feet. Maybe at this moment in time, self-care is taking each day as it comes and not concentrating on anything other than your own and your family's health and wellbeing. Or maybe you've spent the last few weeks or months neglecting your own self-care and you're ready to start implementing some rituals into your routine.

Take a moment

First, reflect on how far you have come! You are doing a wonderful job. Now think about what you need to achieve a more balanced life. Is it about taking a regular break from home and work responsibilities? Spending some alone time with your partner? Is it ensuring you nurture your body with wholesome food or an exercise routine that gives you a boost?

If you have struggled to find pockets of self-care, now is the time to reconnect with yourself, find out what it is that you enjoy and give yourself the permission to pursue it, no guilt involved.

What would you do if you had 15–30 minutes to yourself today? (That doesn't include housework!)

Remember that self-care should not be a chore! Don't feel like you have to: do it because you feel better and happier and it's your little bit of 'me' time. When you don't enjoy something, you probably won't make the time for it. For example, running 5 km is a great goal but if you don't enjoy it, then you are very unlikely to commit long term.

Think of some activities that you genuinely enjoy *and* that make you feel good?

WHY IS SELF-CARE SO IMPORTANT?

- Self-care can enable you to be better equipped in looking after your baby, your family and, importantly, yourself. You cannot pour from an empty cup.

- It can reframe how you view the challenges of motherhood. Self-care can help you to evaluate what you need to change to make this time easier for yourself, when to let go of certain expectations or pressures (both internally and externally), and how you might approach a situation differently next time.

- Self-care allows you to recognise how you are feeling and find time to develop ways to help you cope with stress, challenging situations, birth trauma or parental burnout.

- Self-care teaches us that we don't need to self-sacrifice. You CAN have both time with your baby and time for yourself.

- By implementing self-care rituals into your life, you are also teaching your children about the importance of self-care, and showing them the building blocks for resilience.

You cannot pour from an empty cup.

SELF-CARE CAN . . .

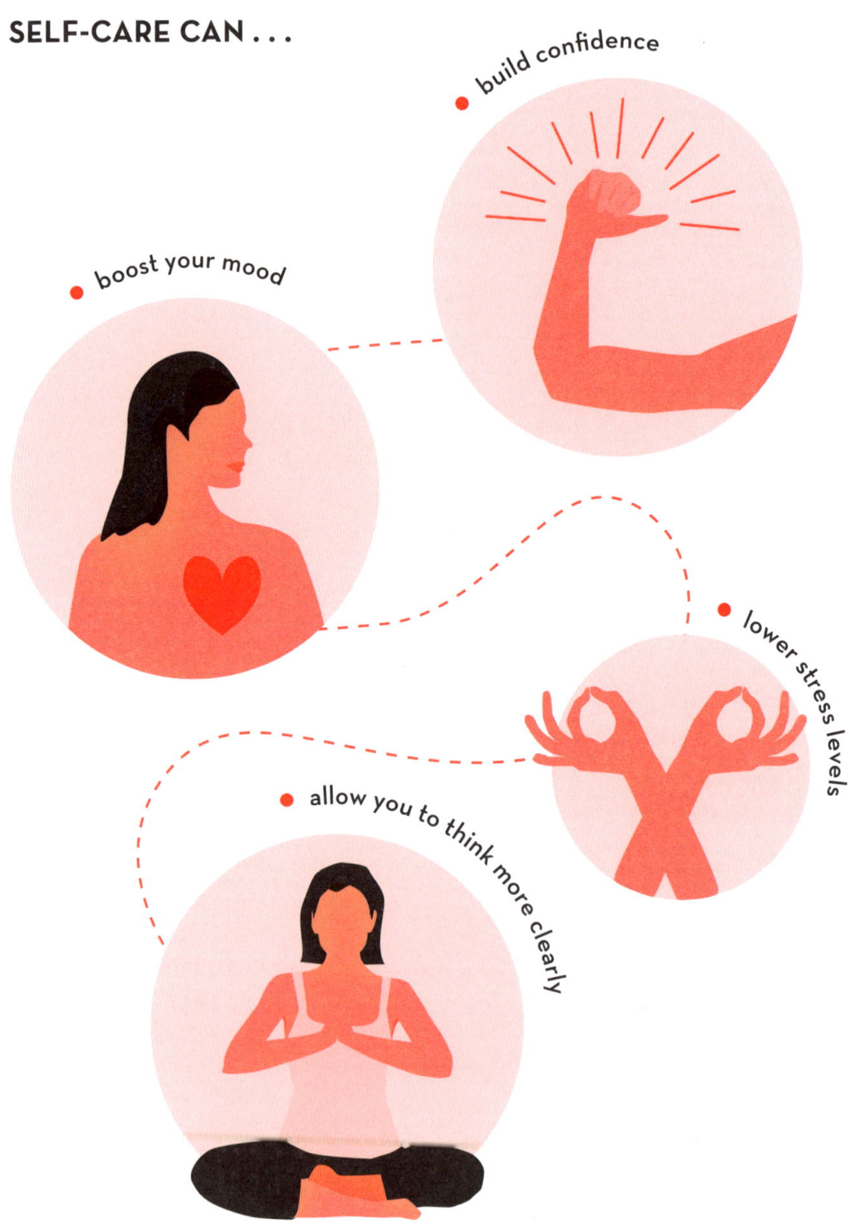

help you to connect with your baby
support you when you are tired and run down
zZz
zzz
zzz
lift your energy levels
and promote self-esteem.

The mental load

The mental load of motherhood is the invisible work, intangible tasks and everyday duties that we carry on our shoulders.

You are not alone. All mothers will share this experience at some point in their parenting journey. This load will inevitably wear us down if we don't make the space and time to pause and enjoy moments of solitude, as well as togetherness as a family.

As parents, we are presented with daily challenges, from home maintenance, financial responsibilities and meal planning to managing our career, our intimate relationship and our extended family. It is a lot to juggle. Some days it can feel all-encompassing.

When you're feeling overwhelmed by the mental load, remind yourself of the times you feel full of hope and excitement for the future and all you have achieved, even in exhaustion! We tend to be hard on ourselves and not give ourselves credit when it is deserved. Remember the joy and laughter that still flourishes in the chaos, and the beauty of creating a family and watching your children grow.

Most importantly, take intentional time to offer yourself care in any way you can. This will help you to acknowledge and reduce your mental load – and also find ways to redistribute it.

It's time to acknowledge, reduce and share the mental load.

How to self-care

There are no right or wrong ways to self-care. It is multi-dimensional and individual to you and your needs. Essentially, self-care is anything that empowers you to feel good and be present in the moment.

We each have our own story to tell; this is what makes us who we are. Consequently, there is no one-size-fits-all approach when it comes to self-care either.

Self-care supports us in times of change – and babies inevitably change our lives. Know that things will continue to change over time. As your baby grows, there will be more windows of opportunity to follow passions and explore new possibilities.

Self-care doesn't need to cost money. You don't need to buy an expensive face mask or go for a massage once a week. It can be as simple and as powerful as loving yourself not only on the good days but also on the bad ones; honouring yourself and your feelings; and allowing yourself to spend time away from your little ones, free from any guilt.

It may be making a conscious effort to sit down with your partner, rather than stacking the dishwasher, and setting time aside to reconnect and enjoy each other's company, conversation and shared experience as a parent.

Self-care could be giving yourself permission to nurture your own mind and body, such as joining a team sport again or practising yoga or meditation, or reading a book.

Perhaps it is about saying no to things that don't serve you, and rejecting negativity. It might be about making choices and decisions that are right for you and your family, no matter what others may think.

Self-care might be about asking for help when you need it, and knowing what will help you to get through difficult times and make you feel good on challenging days.

Sometimes self-care is a practical thing that may seem tiny, but can help you reset. Here are some ideas:

- **Change your bed sheets.**
- **Reorganise or declutter a space in the house.**
- **Wear clothes that make you feel good.**
- **Sit outside in the sunshine with your baby or your partner.**
- **Express how you are feeling to a friend or family member.**

You may like to use your self-care time painting, gardening, working with ceramics or creating other art work. It may be that being busy with your hands is a form of mindfulness for you. Our brains can only focus on one thing at a time, so when we engage in an activity that we enjoy we are focused only on that. This allows those other worries, insecurities and expectations to fall to the wayside and helps to regulate our emotions (because, let's be honest, motherhood is an emotional rollercoaster!).

Remember that self-care is different for everyone.

Take a moment

Set an intention for each of the following; it doesn't need to be big or challenging, just honest.

What does looking after your physical health mean to you?

What does looking after your mental and emotional health mean to you?

What does looking after your social health mean to you?

THINGS TO CONSIDER

When you are planning your week ahead, try to create gaps to fit your self-care into your schedule. Write it in your diary or planner to keep yourself accountable. You may like to look at your list of self-care activities on pages 34 and 35 for ideas. Start small – you can always add to your list.

Go gently with yourself and know your limits. Be mindful that there are many external factors that may be contributing to you feeling more vulnerable, exhausted and emotional than usual. These include:

- **sleep deprivation**
- **fatigue and exhaustion**
- **hormonal shifts**
- **breastfeeding concerns**
- **diet and nutrient consumption**
- **relationship difficulties**
- **financial stress**
- **housing changes**
- **grief and loss**
- **pain, related or unrelated to birth.**

Take note of how you're feeling, and learn to recognise when it is time to respond to your needs; this is more important than cleaning the house or working late into the night.

In time, you'll become more aware of what it is that fulfils you, relaxes and calms you, and fills up your cup.

Remember that self-care isn't selfish, nor does it mean you don't love your baby any less. Self-care can help to maintain positive feelings and a sense of wellbeing, or be a tool you reach for when things are challenging and you're struggling.

Let go of . . .

Perfectionism

Each of us is imperfect and that is what makes us unique. No mother is perfect. Relish in your qualities and what makes you a great parent. Remember that your baby and children don't want a perfect parent; they want one that is loving and happy.

Guilt

We all experience this. Be conscious of when you feel guilty and why. Acknowledge these emotions but give yourself permission to not be bound or affected by them.

Self-doubt

Express gratitude for yourself. Believe in yourself: you are parenting in a way that feels right for you and your family.

Self-judgement

Learn from your mistakes, but remind yourself that they don't define you. Take a moment to reflect on how far you've come and speak to yourself with kind words.

Trying to control everything

Babies are unpredictable at times and it's impossible to control every situation or emotion. Enjoy living in the moment and seeing the positive things that are happening. This may help you to feel in control of how you are feeling in the present moment.

Embrace the seasons

With each season comes new changes. Some days feel like you are on a treadmill and there is no end in sight. Other days flow with ease: you have a rhythm and enjoy some balance. Move with the seasons; they are always changing.

Self-care Sunday

Sunday is the best day of my week. I like to think of it as a day to recharge, plan for the week, spend time with my family and set aside a little window of time for something special for me, even if it is simply to sit down and read a book undisturbed.

Think about the activities that bring you joy and set an intention of finding 'bursts' of time for self-care each Sunday.

Aim to choose something that is a low-stress activity and helps with relaxation, rather than doing the dishes, catching up on washing or tidying up around the house. Those things can wait. That said, you may be the kind of person that takes enjoyment from doing a gentle declutter over the weekend and this helps you to start the week fresh. That is okay too!

Suggestions for a month of Sundays . . .

Self-care Sunday: Week 1

- Start a new book.
- Listen to music.
- Pop a face mask on and take a moment to pause.
- Go for a walk in nature.

Self-care Sunday: Week 2

- Take a bath with some epsom salts to soothe those aching muscles.
- Paint or do something crafty.
- Enjoy a dinner date with your partner.
- Draw up a meal plan for your week ahead.
- Meditate.

Self-care Sunday: Week 3

- Cultivate a new hobby.
- Follow one of your favourite workouts.
- Listen to a podcast.
- Turn off your devices for 24 hours – take a break from socials and have a digital-free day.

Self-care Sunday: Week 4

- Watch a movie or TV show.
- Do a form of exercise you enjoy.
- Catch up with a friend or family member.
- Bake for the week ahead.
- Make a self-care playlist.

Don't forget to include some pampering!

Giving yourself that little bit of tender love, care and indulgence is always a good idea. This might mean blocking out the time every so often to get your hair cut, or enjoy a facial or a massage. There are cost-effective ways to pamper yourself at home. Try a sheet mask or facial, soaking your feet in bath salts or painting your nails. Relax and enjoy the pause. Your body has grown and birthed a new life – make time to reward it with rest!

Always find the time to do things that make you happy.

28-day self-care reset

Make time over the next four weeks to actively pursue self-care, each and every day. Consistently finding time for yourself over this period can help instil self-care as a long-term habit. Take note of how you feel at the beginning and end of the Reset.

Before you begin, choose your self-care practices. Here are some ideas to get you started:

- Have a warm shower.
- Put on a hair mask.
- Read a magazine.
- Cook your favourite lunch.
- Spend some time in nature.
- Start a knitting or sewing project.
- Phone a friend.
- Write in a journal.
- Listen to music that makes you feel happy.
- Go for a wander.

You can also follow the Reset program over the page.

Feel free to make your own list, customised to your own needs and preferences. Remember: there is no right or wrong.

28-DAY SELF-CARE RESET

	Monday	Tuesday	Wednesday
Week 1	Have a bath or warm shower and wash your hair	Read the first chapter of a new book	Cook your favourite meal
Week 2	Go outside and enjoy the sunshine for 20 minutes	Put on a face mask and lie down	Make space for 20 minutes to read your book
Week 3	Take some time in nature – your garden, a nearby park or in the bush	Bake something delicious	Do a craft activity that makes you smile
Week 4	Do some stretching and/or yoga for 30 minutes	Spend 30 minutes enjoying your favourite hobby	Go for a walk with a friend

Thursday	Friday	Saturday	Sunday
Take some time in nature – your garden, a nearby park or in the bush	Spend 15 minutes enjoying your favourite hobby	Start a DIY home project	Listen to music that soothes you for 20 minutes
Continue working on your DIY home project	Meditate for 20 minutes	Go for a walk with your baby	Listen to a podcast or audiobook that you enjoy
Meditate for 25 minutes	Make space for 20 minutes to read your book	Put on a hair mask and relax	Take some extra time to carefully massage moisturiser into your face and body
Make space for 20 minutes to read your book	Go outside and enjoy the sunshine for 20 minutes	Do a craft activity that makes you happy	Meditate for 30 minutes

Or you can build your own 28-day self-care reset. Remember to start slow and include a variety of activities that will support and nourish you.

	Monday	Tuesday	Wednesday
Week 1			
Week 2			
Week 3			
Week 4			

Thursday	Friday	Saturday	Sunday

Routines for self-care

Self-care helps to ground us, bringing us back to our baseline when life may be feeling overwhelming or stressful. It also acts as a shield to build our resilience for when motherhood can feel too consuming. Many of us tend to cope better when our lives have some set structure. When we have a set time to implement self-care, regulate our heart rates, collect our thoughts and connect with our bodies, we tend to cope better with the ups and downs of parenthood. The great thing about routines and rituals is that you can create them to work for you. Having a routine can be helpful when it comes to arranging self-care time for you and your partner, and ensuring it remains a priority.

Start by acknowledging that self-care could reignite your overall wellbeing, both mentally and physically, and make a commitment to give yourself the opportunity to rebuild your ideas around self-care as a new parent, rather than trying to replicate what you did prior to having a baby.

What realistic rituals can you implement into your life now?

What are three activities that bring you joy?

Now think of ways you can integrate those activities into your daily and weekly routines.

MORNING ROUTINE

Setting your intentions for the day can help to alleviate any stress or anxiety you may be feeling and set the tone for the rest of the day.

If you are a morning person, aim for 10 minutes before your baby wakes in the morning. This timeframe will likely increase as your baby sleeps more and settles into a routine. Rather than using those first 10–20 minutes to scroll through social media or answer emails, choose an activity or task that makes you feel good and helps start your day in a positive way. This can simply be washing your hair or sitting quietly with a cup of tea and your thoughts.

Keep your daily goals achievable and realistic.

Make a daily plan the night before to help manage your expectations and help you to prioritise, particularly if you have more than one child. Keep your daily goals achievable and realistic to your lifestyle. Your expectations may be having a shower, getting out of your loungewear and cooking a healthy meal. You'll be surprised at how good you feel and how much it affects your mood for the day when you have a shower in the morning, wash your face, brush your hair and get dressed!

Remember, when you have little ones, it's the small steps to achieve the bigger goal that matter. Don't ever feel guilty about making time just for you.

EVENING ROUTINE

Have you ever been in the shower and imagined you could hear your baby crying only to realise, once you've done a run out dripping wet, that it was your imagination?

As a new parent, you can feel like you are always alert and constantly aware of your baby. After a very long day of this, it can help to unwind before heading to bed. When you get your baby down for the night, or hand them off to your co-parent, give yourself a chance to take a breath and do something for you before you go to sleep.

This may be having a shower without interruptions. It may be sitting down with a cup of tea and chatting to a family member or friend over the phone. Or you might just really want that space of being alone to hear your own thoughts for a while. Whatever it may be, make it right for you.

Try these ways of winding down:

- **Go slow with your skin-care routine.**
- **Take a long bath.**
- **Listen to calming music.**
- **Read in bed.**
- **Put your phone in another room until tomorrow.**
- **Write down anything you want to remember or your plan for the next day, so you can leave busy thoughts on the page and relax your mind.**

The baby bubble

The first 40 days after giving birth is such a special time, sometimes called the 'baby bubble'. Whether it is your first, second or third baby, this bubble is beautiful and should be cherished.

As your hormones settle and you navigate these early days, you may experience an array of emotions. This is the perfect opportunity to practise being kind to yourself. Try to avoid placing any pressures or expectations on yourself during this time.

This transitional season of life is all about learning to trust your intuition. Babies are pretty good at telling us what they need, and every baby is unique, so learn what feels right for you and your baby.

Take the time to enjoy this chapter as a family. Cherish these moments and days because they really do go so quickly. Babies are the best timewasters of all!

SIMPLE WAYS TO PROTECT AND ENJOY YOUR BABY BUBBLE

- Give yourself time to recover from the birth.
- Have uninterrupted time with your baby and your partner – let family and friends know that you will be in touch when you're ready for visitors.
- Enjoy lots of skin-to-skin time with your baby.
- Don't feel any pressure to plan anything.
- When you're feeling ready, aim to get out for a walk or some fresh air every day.
- Rest when you need to.
- Dedicate some time for yourself; not only will you feel good, your partner will enjoy some one-on-one time with your new baby.

Nurture your growth as a mother.

Your self-care toolkit

A self-care toolkit contains things that you like to use in your self-care regime. It can make self-care accessible and habitual, encouraging you to use your self-care toolkit each day or week. Or it can be a go-to for when you've got a small window of downtime and need some nurturing and comfort.

I frequently use my own self-care toolkit when I am feeling overwhelmed or I need a little unwinding in the evenings. I wish this was something I knew about pre-pregnancy and when my babies were little – but it's never too late to start one.

I've listed some ideas over the page or you can of course make your own list, customised to your specific needs and preferences. As always, there is no right or wrong.

YOUR SELF-CARE TOOLKIT

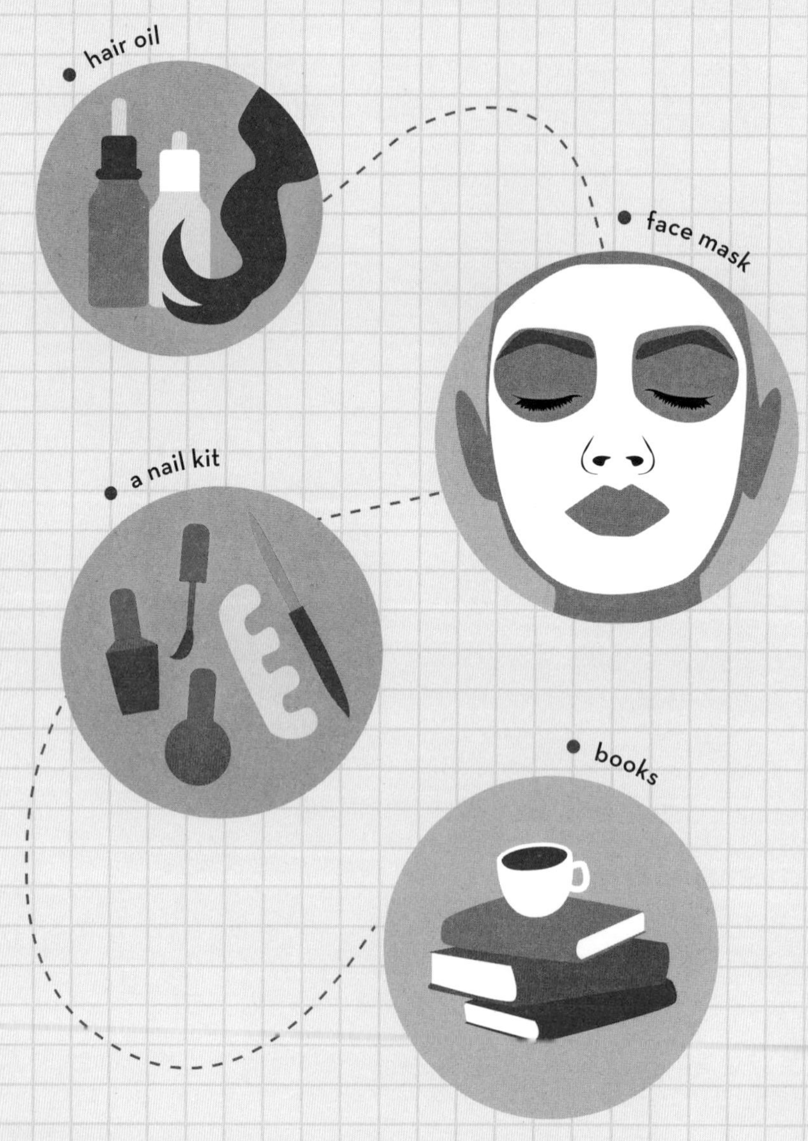

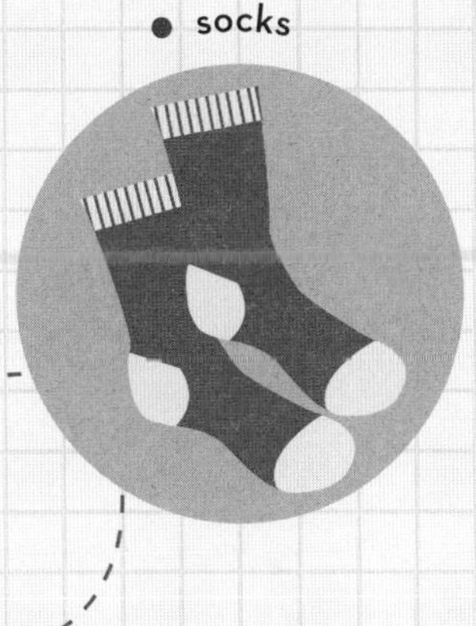

- hot water bottle (perfect for if you've had your baby in the carrier and your back is feeling sore)
- podcast list or music playlist.

Essential oils to try . . .

For sleep

- lavender
- ylang ylang
- chamomile

For lifting your mood

- lavender
- lemon
- rose
- sandalwood

For energy

- lavender
- geranium
- grapefruit
- patchouli

PART 1

Physical self-care

Movement

Exercise

Exercise is a great way to boost overall wellbeing. We know that it releases endorphins and peptides that make us feel good, and it can also help to reduce pain. While your favourite spin class may not be an option right now, it is still possible to incorporate exercise into your weekly self-care routine.

Start small and go slowly. Exercise doesn't have to look like it did pre-pregnancy. Make sure your expectations are manageable, especially in the early postpartum period. Carrying a baby and giving birth is a huge achievement and we experience a significant physical change, as well as the mental and emotional shifts.

Allow your body to heal after birth. Be kind to yourself, move mindfully and prepare a realistic timeframe, rather than pushing yourself to complete that intense hour-long workout you favoured before pregnancy. There is no rush: go at your own pace. The time will come when you can return to that workout, I promise!

It's also important to be aware of any physical issues like abdominal separation, urinary incontinence, or pain you may be experiencing. Always seek support from a health professional, such as your doctor or a physiotherapist, before you engage in any strenuous activity.

Allow your body to heal after birth.

You might begin with some gentle yoga when your baby is napping or a walk with the pram first thing after breakfast, before moving on to higher intensity exercise, such as running or a gym workout.

It can feel difficult to summon the motivation to exercise, particularly when you're tired. Time is so valuable when you have a baby to care for and this can often feel like a barrier to exercising. Rather than reaching for the laundry basket or doing the dishes, try to allow yourself that time to exercise, in the form that feels right for you.

Remember, exercise doesn't have to be scary, intense or long. It can simply be going for a walk, doing an online workout in your living room or joining a mums and bubs class, such as Pilates or yoga. Exercising in a social setting can help to boost your motivation levels and is a great opportunity to meet other parents and form a network of new friends.

And if you have older kids, consider turning exercise into a game to keep them entertained while also getting your heart rate up. Depending on their age, you could do hopscotch, an obstacle course or a dance class on YouTube, or head to the park or beach for some energetic fun and fresh air.

EXERCISING WITH YOUR BABY

- Plan your exercise routine around your baby's nap times.
- Try an at-home online class, such as Pilates, stretching, yoga or a no equipment workout – there are many free options on YouTube, run by reputable health professionals.
- Create your own walking group with other parents or friends.
- Find a local workout group that caters to mums and bubs, such as a gym with a creche or group training that offers babysitting.
- Join a friend and take turns watching/playing with the babies while you each do a workout routine, or swim laps in the local pool.
- Put your baby in a carrier or in the pram to exercise, whether that's a walk at the beach, in a nature reserve or just around your neighbourhood.

Yoga and stretching

These gentle stretches may assist with common issues post-birth, such as a sore neck and back from feeding or sore hips from carrying little ones, as well as helping to strengthen your stomach muscles.

- **Delts and pecs stretch:**
  Hold your arms out in front, with your elbows bent to the sides, as if you are holding a plate with two hands. Keep the shoulders relaxed. With palms facing upwards, slowly move from the elbow to the tips of the fingers in an outwards direction.

- **Hip stretches and release:**
  Lie flat on the floor with legs at a 90-degree angle. Pull one leg off the floor and fold your other leg over, with the ankle placed flat on your knee. Pull your knee in towards your chest to get that hip release.

Use a foam roller to stretch and release any pain in your thighs, upper and lower back.

- **Bridges for pelvic floor and lower back:**
  Roll up through your spine, holding your hips in the air, and curl back down to release. Don't forget to engage your core and activate your pelvic floor muscles.

- **Toe taps:**
  Lie flat on your back, with your legs bent and feet flat on the floor. Pull your stomach in, as you would with a pelvic floor exercise, and lift each leg slowly up into a 90-degree angle. Release and repeat.

- **Relaxation:**
  Try child's pose or simply lie on your back on the floor.

Taking care of **yourself** is taking care of your **baby.**

5-minute yoga mini-flow

Starting and/or ending the day with this routine can help to regulate your heart rate, slow your breathing, stretch your muscles and connect you with your body.

Slow down and connect with your body.

- 60-second downward dog
- 20-second upward dog
- 20-second standing backbend
- 40-second forward fold.

Setting up a feeding station

Early on, a baby's pattern tends to be feed and sleep on repeat. You can spend a lot of time feeding! Set up your own station to make the experience comfortable and enjoyable. Ideas for creating a relaxing and practical space include:

- a comfortable chair
- some healthy, non-perishable snacks
- tissues and wipes
- a water bottle
- muslin wraps (and breast pads, if breastfeeding)
- a phone charger
- some face cream and a hairbrush
- a soft nightlight for the evenings
- pillows (and/or a breastfeeding pillow) and a blanket
- a fan for warm evenings.

If you have another little one, you can include some toys and books for them to stay entertained while you feed.

Relax those shoulders

While you're feeding or cradling your baby, focus on how your shoulders and jaw are positioned. Ideally, try to keep your shoulders down and not hunched, as this can cause headaches and/or neck and back pain. When stressed or overwhelmed, you might reflexively clench your jaw, so make a specific effort to relax your face and jaw.

Yesterday was heavy. Put it down.

Facial massage

Massage activates your sympathetic nervous system, which leads to feelings of tranquility and relaxation. You can choose to massage with your hands and fingers or, if you prefer, you can use a gua sha. This is a calming ritual for your evenings and a great way to hydrate your skin.

Pour a few drops of your preferred face oil, coconut oil or rosehip oil into your palm.

Cover your face with the oil, then, starting at your chin, work your fingers in an upward motion.

From either side of your nose, push your fingers in an outward motion towards your ears and side of face.

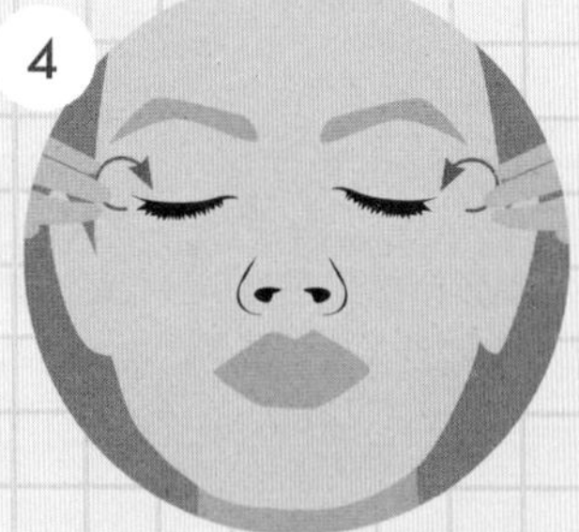

Massage gently into your temples in a circular motion.

Massage, following the direction of your eyebrows and back to your temples.

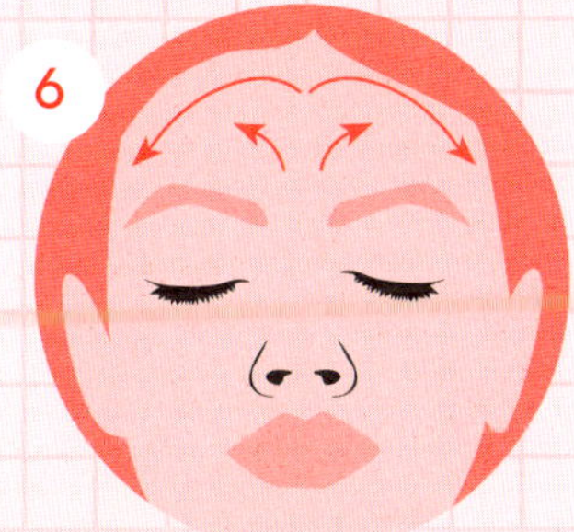

Work your way to your forehead and massage towards your hairline.

Using four fingers, sweep in an upwards motion along your neck up to your chin.

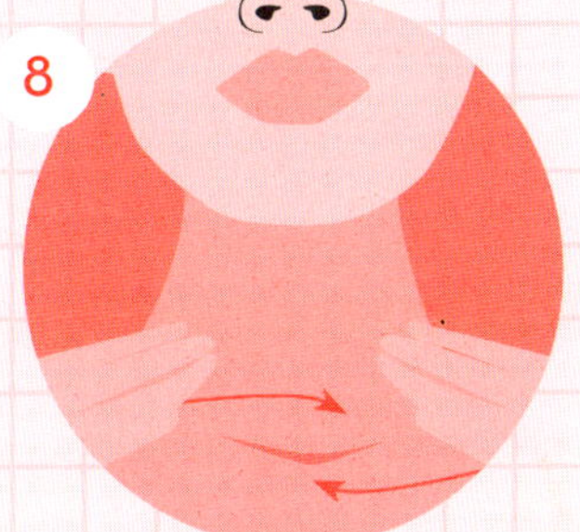

Don't forget to massage around your decolletage area with some extra oil.

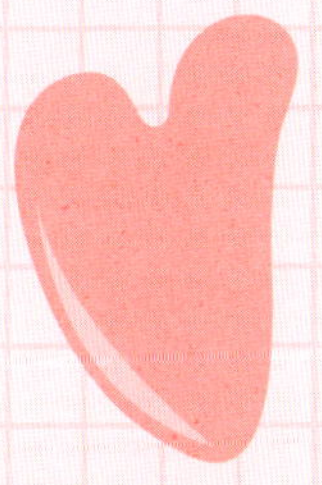

Gua sha is a traditional Chinese tool used to stroke the skin on your face. It is said to improve circulation and reduce fine lines and wrinkles. It is also very relaxing!

You are not alone.

Pelvic floor exercises

You've probably heard of your pelvic floor and how beneficial strengthening it can be after having a baby. The pressures of pregnancy and childbirth (no matter what type of birth) can put you at risk of pelvic floor muscle dysfunction.

Some women experience leakage when jumping, running, sneezing, coughing, laughing and lifting weights. All these activities place pressure on the pelvic floor. Other women might experience pain, vaginal heaviness, trouble emptying their bowels or difficulty making it to the toilet in time. These can all be symptoms of a pelvic floor not functioning correctly. Pelvic floor muscle dysfunction is very common, and you are not alone. These symptoms can be helped with a targeted treatment plan: consult your ob-gyn, doctor or pelvic floor physiotherapist for help.

Many women ask the question: Will it ever get better? The answer is yes, with the right pelvic floor treatment, which – like with any muscle – takes time. A great place to start for everyone is to create that connection from brain to muscle by spending time bringing awareness to that muscle, and the subtleties that come with squeezing and relaxing it.

Q&A

WITH PHYSIOTHERAPIST **CAITLIN DUNSFORD**

Caitlin Dunsford is a mother, physiotherapist and founder of The Pelvic Floor Project.

What is pelvic floor dysfunction and what are some of the symptoms?

Pelvic floor dysfunction relates to a pelvic floor muscle that is overactive, underactive, poorly coordinated, tight or weak.

Symptoms can include:

- **bladder urgency, or needing to wee many times a day (a typical range for an average female is four to seven times)**
- **incomplete bladder or bowel emptying**
- **constipation**
- **feeling of vaginal heaviness**
- **urinary incontinence or fecal incontinence**
- **and painful sex.**

When should I see someone about my pelvic floor?

As soon as you notice your symptoms, especially if they bother you or impact your life. Make an appointment with your GP, ob-gyn or a pelvic floor therapist. It may be that when you see them, there aren't any issues identified and you learn a bit about your body and walk out more empowered than when you walked in.

Or it may be that your symptoms that were bothering you can be fixed by some simple conservative management strategies, and you get your quality of life back.

What are some simple exercises you recommend to help with the pelvic floor soon after giving birth?

Pelvic Floor Muscle Training is a term for exercises involving your pelvic floor. It involves strength, stretching and coordination work. Soon after giving birth, pelvic floor training may look like gentle pulses of your pelvic floor to improve activation and awareness. After one to two weeks, you may progress to some holds, two to three times for three sets. You can then try increasing by a second each week, up until your baby is six weeks old.

We usually advise women to squeeze their anus, like they are holding in wind, as this visualisation usually results in an improved squeeze of the pelvic floor. We discourage breath holding or 'sucking in' of the tummy. You can do these simple exercises lying down, sitting or standing up. Around the four-week mark, we might add some mobility and whole pelvis strengthening exercises, things like cat/cow, pelvic tilts, bridges, adductor squeezes and breathing exercises on your hands and knees.

Pelvic floor training usually looks like 8–12 weeks of squeeze-and-relax style exercises in positions such as lying or standing or sitting, with three sets of 8–12 reps, usually daily.

DID YOU KNOW?

One in three women after giving birth experience pelvic floor symptoms, including leakage when laughing, coughing and sneezing.

How long does it usually take to notice an improvement in my pelvic floor with regular strengthening exercises?

It is worth noting that natural recovery of physiological processes has some effect on the improvement of incontinence, specifically in the postpartum period.

Research has shown that by doing pelvic floor exercises regularly, you can expect to see results anywhere from the four–six week mark, with best results taking approximately 10–12 weeks.

Please note that pelvic floor exercises aren't for everyone! While women should be empowered to exercise in their own homes, it's still important to seek individualised assessment, especially if your symptoms don't get better with simple strategies.

Are there preventative measures I can take before I have another baby?

Yes! Exercise 30 minutes, five days a week, has been shown to reduce the risk of instrumental delivery in the general population of pregnant women, which is a risk factor for pelvic floor dysfunction. Pelvic floor training during the antenatal period reduces urinary incontinence in late pregnancy and in the first year postpartum.

It is important to remember that increased weight is a risk factor of pelvic floor dysfunction.

Perineal massage is also recommended from 34 weeks (earlier or later as prescribed by a midwife or obstetrician). It involves deep pressure and stretching massage using one to two fingers, inserted vaginally and pushing towards the anus, to stretch the perineum in preparation for second stage of labour.

Embrace
your
imperfections.
They
make you,
you!

Sleep and rest

Sleep

Once you give birth, it can be difficult to remember what it was like to get a full night's sleep. You may wonder if you'll enjoy eight hours of uninterrupted slumber ever again. You will!

But in the meantime, sleep deprivation can wreak havoc on your mood, your ability to think clearly, your body and overall wellbeing. Sleep and mental health are so interconnected. The frequent nights of broken sleep and extra fatigue may leave you feeling more irritable than normal, emotionally flat and lacking in energy.

We often spend a lot of time, effort and money on ways to help our babies sleep – particularly if your child doesn't seem to feel the same way about sleep as you do!

What we tend to forget is our own sleep, other than knowing that we desperately want more of it. You can make some adjustments that may help you to get a little more sleep, especially when you need it most, as well as increasing the quality of sleep when quantity may not be an option. Here are some tips and ideas.

Create a screen-free space

Make your bedroom a room purely for sleep and relaxation. Keep devices in another room.

Enjoy a bedtime snack

Warm milk is not just for your baby! It contains an amino acid called tryptophan, which can help to induce sleep. Add a little bit of honey if you're not a fan of the taste of milk on its own. Another natural solution is a handful of pistachios, which contain melatonin and may aid in promoting and preparing your body for sleep.

Listen to calming music

Music has been scientifically proven to have a positive effect neurologically and physiologically when it comes to aiding sleep. Calming and relaxing soft music in the bedroom may help you to wind down after a busy or stressful day, and assist with drifting off to sleep quicker.

Soak up some vitamin D

Getting out into the sunshine for even a small period of time each day can be beneficial for both you and baby. Not only does it encourage your baby's sleep-and-wake cycles, it has some great advantages for your overall wellbeing. Vitamin D increases your absorption of calcium in the body and plays a role in your immune health. This is particularly important for mothers during childbearing years. Vitamin D uptake leads to increased muscle health, heart health and supporting your immune system. The sounds of the ocean, wind or birds along with fresh air can give you that little pick-me-up that you might be craving, and you may find your baby is more settled.

Shower in low light

If you enjoy showering before hopping into bed, try having a shower with low light or a candle. This may help you to wind down and calm your nervous system.

Draw up a sleep-in roster

Organise designated sleep-ins, alternating days for both you and your partner.

MORE WAYS TO IMPROVE YOUR SLEEP

- Plan for a same time bedtime and wake time, even though inevitably you will have wake periods throughout the night.
- Create a relaxing sleep environment, with comfortable pillows and clothing.
- Never bring screens or work into your sleep zone.
- Limit caffeine after noon if you can and choose decaffeinated tea or coffee if you are craving one after lunch.
- Limit alcohol consumption.
- Avoid rigorous exercise right before bed.
- Use meditation or relaxation techniques, such as massage, a warm bath or shower, or yoga or stretching, to help calm the nervous system before sleep, particularly in times of feeling overwhelmed.

Less waking, more snoozing

If your baby is still a newborn and being fed regularly overnight, there are some ways that may allow you to get just that little bit of extra sleep.

- Dreamfeed your baby. This is when you give them a feed at a specific time in the night while they are still partially asleep. This is usually done before you go to bed, to extend the time between feeds so that you can get a good amount of sleep before your baby wakes.
- Create a feeding schedule with your partner, taking turns at feeding intervals.
- Try taking turns preparing the baby for bed. This may be where one parent does the feeding and bath while the other cooks dinner. Alternate each evening. This can make you feel better supported, give you both one-on-one time with your new baby and share parenting responsibilities.
- Use music and/or white noise. Both may help you and your baby fall asleep more easily. It can also assist with masking noise, which in turn could lead to less waking.

Give yourself permission to rest.

Rest

'Sleep when your baby sleeps'. We've all been given this advice, and if you can squeeze in a nap while your baby is asleep, it is a great form of self-care.

On the other hand, while it is a terrific idea, it is often unattainable or difficult if you've got a baby who doesn't nap during the day or if you cannot nap in the daytime. If this is you and sleeping isn't an option, aim instead to take some time to pause and rest. It can do wonders for your mind and body, particularly if you've had several nights of broken sleep.

Rest doesn't need to be about sleep; it can simply be doing something unproductive, lying on the sofa reading or logging off from socials for a while and giving yourself a mental rest.

As a parent, you are the chef, housekeeper, child carer, driver, accountant, teacher, counsellor . . . and the list goes on. You wear so many hats and it's essential to give yourself the kindness and nurturing you deserve, and allow your mind and body to rest, recharge and reenergise.

SOME IDEAS FOR RESTING

- Find a comfortable space in a different room from where your baby is sleeping and simply take time for solitude.
- Do something slow and 'unproductive' – paint your nails, read a book, colour in a picture.
- Meditate or do a body scan.
- Listen to music or a soothing podcast.
- Diffuse some essential oils (see page 45).
- Brew some tea or make a simple, nurturing meal.

Nourishment

Nourishing and fuelling your body with healthy wholefoods is essential self-care. When we eat better, we feel better. Post-birth, it's important to give your body the opportunity to restore its nutrient levels, so that you can feel stronger, have more energy and boost your immune system.

But how do you manage to make a nutritious meal for yourself when you are caring for your baby? Between feeding, cleaning, washing and sleeping (or not), it is often easier to reach for Vegemite toast and make that tenth cup of tea for the day.

Many mothers feel pressure to 'get their body back' or 'bounce back' post-pregnancy. The postpartum period is not an ideal time to start a restrictive diet; in fact, they are generally not recommended as they tend not to provide adequate nutrients for your body and your baby. If you are concerned about weight gain and would like to feel better, book an appointment with a dietician who will help you to develop an eating plan that supports your individual needs during this time.

To eat healthily, you don't need fancy ingredients or to double your food budget. There are subtle changes you can make that give you more nutrients and vitamins, and less of the stuff your body doesn't need.

The problem is that when we are time-poor, we tend to skip meals or grab something on the run. We are all guilty of this! Don't be tough on yourself.

Instead, fill your fridge with healthy options so that when you are fatigued, you've got easy ways to make good choices. And be realistic with your time. Don't expect yourself to be in the kitchen prepping meals all day, or spending hours meal-planning. This is not the time to invite extra pressures into your life!

TOP TIPS FOR NOURISHING YOURSELF

- Aim to eat a healthy breakfast with protein and fibre – if this is all you manage for the day that's okay!
- Avoid screens at mealtimes, as eating while distracted means we are not aware of when we are full, potentially leading to overeating.
- Practise mindful eating – it's a great way to properly enjoy the flavours, smells and textures of the food you are eating and feel satisfied afterwards.
- Have healthy go-to food options ready for those days when you don't feel like making something, or don't have the time.
- Stay hydrated, especially if you're breastfeeding – always keep a water bottle close by.

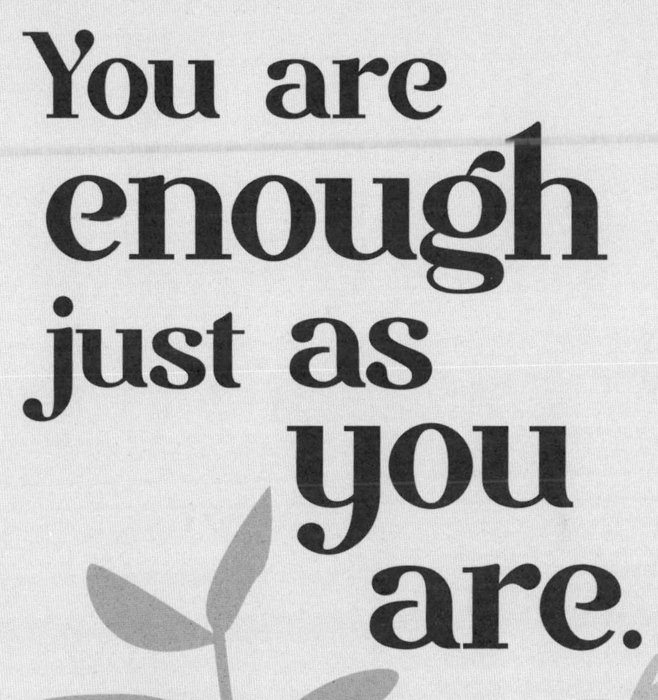
You are
enough
just as
you
are.

Q&A

WITH DIETICIAN **MEAGAN ROSE**

Meagan Rose is a mother of two and a registered practising dietician in Newcastle, NSW.

Are there nutrients that I should increase in my diet after giving birth?

There are a few key nutrients that can be beneficial to your diet after having a baby. These include iron, iodine, folate and B vitamins. Increasing fluids, especially if you are breastfeeding, is beneficial. Try to drink a glass of water every time you sit down to feed your baby.

Overall calorie intake should also increase if you are breastfeeding. Choose nutrient-dense foods and snacks to supplement this increase.

Are there some easy ways to increase my intake/ absorption of iron through food?

To increase your absorption of iron, have vitamin C with iron-rich foods. This can be as simple as having a piece of fruit or glass of juice with a meal.

Some foods can hinder the absorption of iron, such as those containing dairy and caffeine. If you are a coffee or tea drinker, try waiting 30 minutes before and after iron-rich meals to enjoy these. This also applies if you are taking an iron supplement.

I am hungry often now that I am breastfeeding. Is this normal?

Yes! Breastfeeding increases your energy output and it is recommended that extra calories are consumed. It is suggested that you increase your energy by 500 calories a day or 2000KJ, which is nearly equivalent to one extra meal. A great way to increase your energy intake is to add a few extra snacks into your day. Aim to consume foods that are nutrient-rich and help to fill you up.

Are there foods I should avoid while breastfeeding?

Alcohol is not recommended when breastfeeding. Likewise, caffeine passes into breastmilk, so it can be beneficial to limit your caffeine intake to two to four cups daily. This includes coffee, tea, hot chocolate and energy drinks.

It's best to limit foods high in salt, added sugar and saturated fats. These foods provide additional calories, but they tend to be lacking in nutrients.

Can you suggest some healthy foods that I can eat on-the-go?

My top foods for busy parents include yoghurt, nuts, fruit, good-quality muesli bars, smoothies, overnight oats, cheese and crackers, boiled eggs and tinned tuna.

SIMPLE FOOD SWAPS

Instead of:	Try:
White bread	Wholegrain bread or rye bread
Soft drinks	Sparkling water with a squeeze of fresh lemon juice
Fatty meats, such as bacon, sausages, and mince that has a high fat content	Lean meats such as kangaroo, skinless chicken or turkey. If you are consuming red meat, cut off any excess fat
Chips	Wholegrain crackers
Full-fat dairy	Low-fat dairy
Coffee	Herbal tea

Key nutrients for new mums

Iron

It isn't uncommon for women to have lower iron levels post-pregnancy. Iron helps to carry oxygen around the body.

When we are low in iron, we may have symptoms such as fatigue, feeling weak, chest pain or a fast heart rate, cold extremities (hands and feet), headaches, dizziness and light-headedness.

During pregnancy and post-birth, our iron requirements are increased. If you are worried about your iron levels, visit your GP who can order a simple blood test to check.

If iron supplements are recommended, try taking them 30–40 minutes before or after foods containing dairy or caffeine to encourage better absorption.

Foods that contain iron:

- lean meats
- green leafy vegetables (the darker, the better)
- beans and legumes
- and iron-fortified cereals.

Protein

Protein is such an essential nutrient and plays a role in almost every cell in our bodies. It helps with repair, growth and development, and gives us the energy our bodies need to function. Foods high in protein include lean meats, eggs, fish and seafood, dairy products, legumes, nuts and seeds.

Vitamin D

Vitamin D plays a vital role in helping the body to absorb important nutrients such as calcium and magnesium. Vitamin D can be found in fatty fish, fortified foods such as cereals and soy milk, some dairy products and eggs.

B vitamins

B vitamins are crucial for our body to function optimally and enable the creation of new blood cells. They are also essential for converting the food we consume into energy. They are found in milk, cheese, eggs, liver, lean meats, green leafy vegetables, oysters, fish, avocado and citrus fruits such as oranges.

Calcium

Calcium is important for not only breastfeeding mothers but all women. If you are vegan, make sure you check labels to ensure that you are selecting products that contain calcium to reduce the risk of becoming deficient. Calcium can be found in milk, cheese and yoghurt and other dairy products, some soy products, and green leafy vegetables.

Folate and Iodine

You probably remember your midwife or ob-gyn talking to you about folate and iodine in pregnancy. Folate and iodine continue to be important in the postpartum period, as they assist with thyroid hormones in our bodies. These can be found in green leafy vegetables, including broccoli, cabbage, kale and spinach, peanuts, legumes and beans, liver, and some breakfast cereals. You may talk to your healthcare provider about continuing to take your prenatal vitamins. The best sources of iodine are seaweed, seafood including fish, and eggs. There is also iodine in some dairy products.

DID YOU KNOW?

When cooked and then cooled, pasta, rice and potatoes develop resistant starch, which is beneficial for digestion, gut health and lowering blood sugar levels. So make extra and use it to bulk up your next salad.

Don't forget to celebrate the small wins.

Easy savoury snacks

Guacamole and wholemeal crackers

Fruit

Tuna

Celery and nut butter

Easy sweet treats

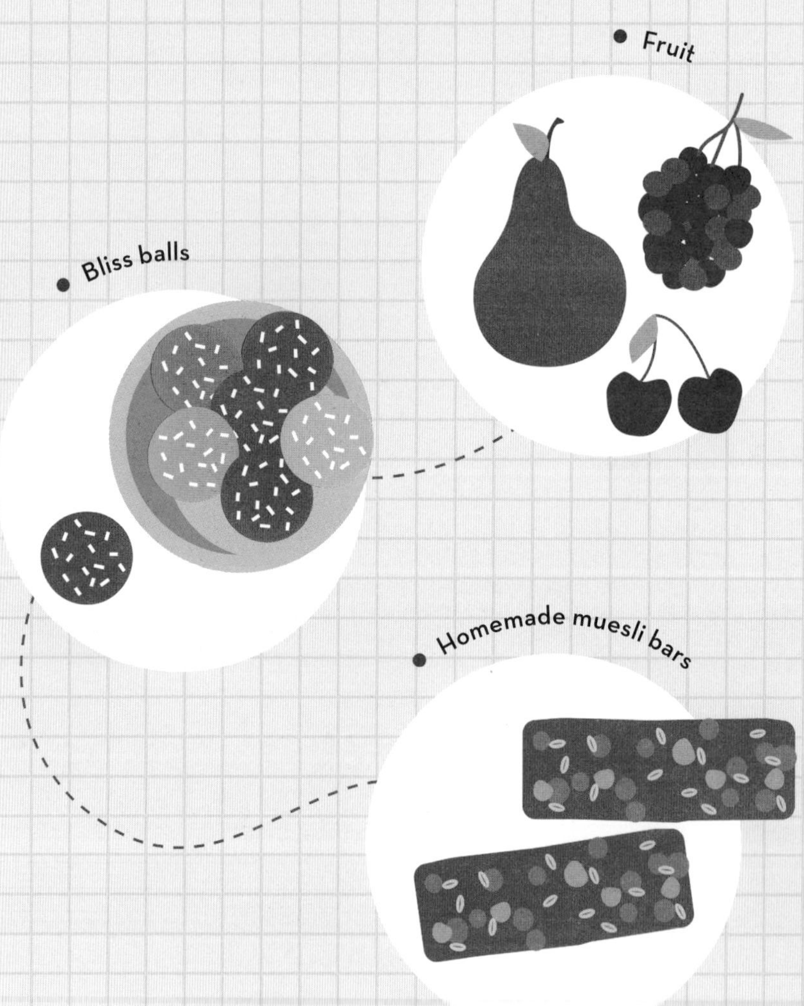

Smoothie
Chia pudding
Fruit salad and yoghurt
Dark chocolate

Recipes

Breakfast ideas

- Omelette
- Porridge with stewed apples and pears
- Quick scrambled eggs with avocado and baby spinach

Things on toast

- Boiled egg and toast with baby spinach
- Peanut butter, sliced banana on toast

- Avocado with cheese and tomato on sourdough or wholegrain toast

Easy Bircher muesli

SERVES 2

1 cup rolled oats
1 cup apple juice
1 teaspoon ground cinnamon
Grated apple, or berries (optional)
1 tablespoon natural Greek yoghurt
½ cup pitted medjool dates, chopped
1 tablespoon almond meal
1 teaspoon LSA mix
Honey (optional)

Combine the oats, juice and cinnamon in a glass jar or container, stir, cover and place in the fridge overnight.

Serve the muesli in a bowl with the fruit, yoghurt, dates, almond meal and LSA with a drizzle of honey, if desired.

Easy smoothies for fast pick-me-ups

Pre-prepare and pour your smoothie mixes into large ice-cube trays, then store in the freezer. When you need a smoothie on the go, add two cubes and some coconut water to a blender, whiz and your breakfast is ready. If you are breastfeeding and would like to include brewer's yeast in your diet, add 1 teaspoon. Frozen cauliflower will boost nutrients and yield a creamier smoothie. Vanilla protein powder can be used as an additional protein source; a whey-free plant-based protein is best for digestion. Many contain probiotics, magnesium and amino acids. Look for one with the fewest ingredients and the least amount of sugar.

Banana smoothie

½ cup frozen banana pieces, or 1 banana, chopped
1 tablespoon vanilla protein powder
1 ½ tablespoons shredded coconut
1 tablespoon chia seeds
1 cup milk (nut milk or cow's milk)
½ cup coconut water

Blend all ingredients together in a blender until smooth.

Coconut bliss smoothie

½ cup frozen banana pieces, or 1 banana
½ cup frozen coconut pieces
1 teaspoon peanut butter
1 tablespoon vanilla protein powder
½ cup milk (nut milk or cow's milk)
½ cup coconut water

Blend all ingredients together in a blender until smooth.

Green smoothie

½ banana, chopped
¼ avocado
¼ zucchini (preferably frozen)
1 teaspoon vanilla protein powder
1 cup milk (nut milk or cow's milk)

Blend all ingredients together in a blender until smooth.

Breakfast smoothie

1 banana, chopped
2 tablespoons rolled oats
1 teaspoon chia seeds
1 tablespoon almond meal
1 scoop vanilla protein powder
1 tablespoon natural peanut butter
1 cup water

Blend all ingredients together in a blender until smooth.

Lunch ideas

Soups

These are great to make ahead, freeze, reheat and serve with crusty bread.

Minestrone is the perfect soup to make when you've got vegetables in the fridge that need to be used up, such as carrots that have gone a little soft. It is easy and simple to make – throw all the vegetables in a pot and add some stock, a tin of tomatoes and risoni or macaroni. Bulk out with a can of your favourite beans for a protein hit. Also try: **cauliflower soup**, **tomato soup** and **pumpkin soup**.

Toppings for crispbreads or sourdough

- **Smoked salmon and avocado with dill**
- **Tahini and Vegemite**
- **Avocado and a fried egg**
- **Cucumber, tomato and cheese**
- **Tomato chutney, lettuce and avocado**
- **Avocado, tomato, feta and balsamic glaze**
- **Smashed avocado with sprouts, chives and lemon**

MEAT-FREE MEALS

Mixing up your weekly mealplan to include some meat-free meals can be great for the budget and also beneficial in forming a more balanced diet. Alternative sources of protein, such as beans and legumes, are high in fibre and good for your gut. Preparing meat-free meals also encourages you to boost your vegetable intake – another excellent reason to enjoy them more often!

Dinner

Sweet potato tacos

SERVES 2

1 large sweet potato, cubed
1 tablespoon olive oil
6 small wholewheat tortillas (or wraps)
¼ cup Greek-style yoghurt, to serve
Sprinkle of chopped coriander, to serve

Toppings

1 cup chopped lettuce
½ small red capsicum, diced
2 tomatoes, diced
1 cucumber, sliced

Preheat the oven to 200°C (180°C fan-forced).

Spread the sweet potato on a baking tray and drizzle with the olive oil. Roast for 30 minutes or until soft.

Wrap the tortillas in foil and place in the oven for 3–5 minutes to warm.

Arrange the sweet potato and toppings on each tortilla. Serve with the Greek yoghurt and coriander.

Kangaroo tacos

SERVES 2–4

8 soft tacos
1 tablespoon olive oil
1 onion, diced
500 g kangaroo mince
1 cup canned brown lentils, drained and rinsed
1 cup finely sliced lettuce
1 avocado, mashed
2 tomatoes, diced
1 cup grated cheese
Sour cream (optional)

Mexican spice mix
1 tablespoon ground coriander
1 tablespoon paprika
1 tablespoon ground cumin
1 tablespoon garlic powder
1 teaspoon ground cinnamon
1 teaspoon sea salt
1 teaspoon chilli powder (optional)

Preheat the oven to 180°C (160°C fan-forced).

Combine all the Mexican spice mix ingredients in a bowl and mix well. Set aside. Wrap the tacos in foil and place in the oven for 5 minutes to warm.

Heat the olive oil in a frying pan over medium heat. Add the onion and 2 tablespoons Mexican spice mix and fry for 2 minutes or until fragrant. Add the kangaroo mince and fry, stirring occasionally, for 2 minutes or until the meat is browned through.

Add the lentils to the pan and cook for a further minute, until warmed through. Remove from the heat.

Divide the kangaroo mixture between the warm tacos, top with the lettuce, avocado, tomato and cheese, and finish with ½ teaspoon of sour cream per taco, if desired.

Lamb cutlets with potatoes and greens

SERVES 2

2 large potatoes, cubed
2 tablespoons olive oil
1 garlic clove, crushed
2 teaspoons rosemary leaves
4–6 lamb cutlets, french trimmed
1 bunch broccolini, trimmed
½ cup frozen peas
Boiling water
Mint sauce, to serve (optional)

Preheat the oven to 200°C (180°C fan-forced). Line a baking tray with baking paper.

Place the potato in a saucepan, cover with water and bring to the boil. Cook for 15 minutes or until soft. Drain well.

Meanwhile, rub the olive oil, garlic and rosemary into the lamb cutlets and place on the baking tray. Cover with foil and roast for 15 minutes. Remove the lamb cutlets from the oven, turn them, add the parboiled potato around the lamb and roast for another 15 minutes.

Place the broccolini and peas in a heatproof bowl and cover with boiling water. Set aside to blanch for 3 minutes. Drain, refresh with cool water and drain again.

Drizzle the mint sauce, if using, on the lamb and serve with the potato, broccolini and peas.

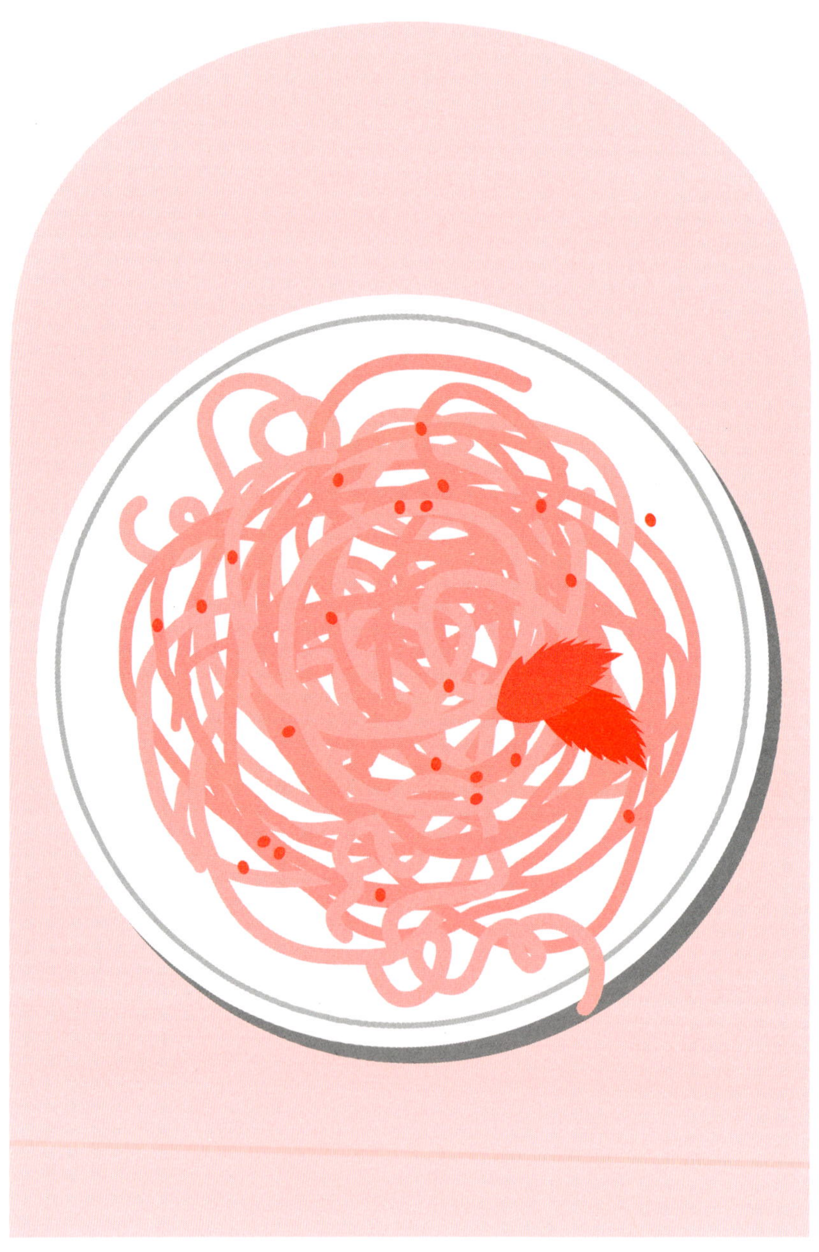

Pesto pasta

SERVES 4

1 bunch basil, leaves picked
2 tablespoons olive oil
1 garlic clove, roughly chopped
¼ cup almond meal
¼ cup grated parmesan
¼ cup frozen peas
500 g wholewheat pasta

Place the basil leaves, olive oil and garlic in a blender and blend until a chunky paste forms.

Add the almond meal and parmesan to the blender and blend until combined. Add the peas and a dash of water and blend for a few minutes or until smooth.

Bring a large pot of lightly salted water to the boil. Add the pasta and cook according to the packet instructions until al dente.

Drain the pasta, return to the pot and place over low heat. Add the pesto, stir to coat the pasta and cook for 1 minute or until warmed through.

Note

You can also freeze this pesto sauce and pull it out when you need a quick meal.

Ginger soy fish and rice

SERVES 2

- 1 cup brown rice
- 2 cups water
- 200 g white fish (snapper or kingfish)
- 1 lemon, sliced
- 1 bunch bok choy, trimmed
- ½ cup topped and tailed green beans
- 1 bunch broccolini, trimmed
- ½ cup snow peas, trimmed
- 2 tablespoons tamari (or soy sauce)
- 2 teaspoons peanut oil
- 2 cm piece of ginger, grated
- 2 spring onions, finely chopped
- 2 tablespoons chopped coriander
- Lime wedges, to serve

Preheat the oven to 200°C (180°C fan-forced). Place the rice in a saucepan, add the water and bring to the boil. Reduce the heat to low and simmer for 25 minutes or until all the water is absorbed. Keep warm.

Place the fish on a piece of baking paper, top with the lemon and roast for 10 minutes or until, when pierced with a fork, the flesh is no longer translucent. Cut the fish into 3 cm pieces. Place the bok choy, beans and broccolini in a steamer basket over a saucepan of simmering water, cover and steam for 3–4 minutes. Add the snow peas and steam for another 1 minute.

Combine the tamari and peanut oil in a bowl. Divide the rice between plates and top with the fish. Add the vegetables, sprinkle on the ginger, spring onion and coriander and drizzle on the tamari and peanut oil. Serve with the lime wedges.

Chicken san choy bow

SERVES 2–4

- 2 teaspoons peanut oil
- 1 garlic clove, crushed
- 2 cm piece of ginger, finely chopped
- 500 g chicken mince
- 2 tablespoons tamari (or soy sauce)
- 1 tablespoon oyster sauce
- 2 teaspoons sesame oil
- 1 carrot, sliced into batons
- 3 spring onions, finely sliced
- 1 baby cos lettuce, leaves separated into cups
- ¼ cup crushed peanuts

Heat the peanut oil in a frying pan over medium–high heat. Add the garlic and ginger and stir-fry for 1–2 minutes or until fragrant. Add the chicken mince and cook, stirring, for 3 minutes or until just cooked through.

Combine the tamari, oyster sauce and sesame oil in a bowl. Add to the pan and stir. Add the carrot and stir-fry for another 2 minutes. Stir in the spring onion and cook for a further 1 minute.

Place the lettuce cups on plates, spoon on the chicken mixture and sprinkle on the crushed peanuts to serve.

Note

For a nut-free meal, use vegetable oil for cooking and sprinkle with sesame seeds to serve.

Quick salads for any time of day

Speedy Niçoise

SERVES 2

2 eggs, at room temperature
95 g can tuna in olive oil or spring water, drained
1 spring onion, finely chopped
1 carrot, chopped
1/2 cup halved cherry tomatoes
1/2 cup sliced, topped and tailed green beans
1/2 avocado, sliced
1 cup baby spinach leaves
1/4 cup sliced pitted black olives

Dressing

1 tablespoon extra virgin olive oil
1 teaspoon dijon mustard
1 tablespoon apple cider vinegar
Pinch of sea salt and freshly ground black pepper

Bring a small saucepan of water to the boil. Add the eggs and cook for 7 minutes. Set aside until cool enough to handle, then peel.

Meanwhile, combine all the dressing ingredients in a small bowl and whisk well.

Place the tuna, spring onion, carrot, cherry tomatoes, beans, avocado, spinach and olives in a bowl. Drizzle on the dressing and gently toss. Cut the eggs in half and add to the salad. Serve.

Note

Eggs are packed full of nutrients, including proteins, good fats which are known to reduce cholesterol, vitamin D, B vitamins and omega 3 fatty acids. Choose free-range eggs.

Roast veggie salad

SERVES 2

3-4 mixed root vegetables (potato, sweet potato, onion, pumpkin), cubed
2 teaspoons olive oil
Sea salt
2 asparagus spears, woody ends trimmed, cut into bite-sized pieces
½ avocado, sliced
1 cup shredded lettuce
1 carrot, chopped
1 tomato, sliced
1 teaspoon sunflower seeds (optional)
50 g feta, crumbled (optional)

Preheat the oven to 180°C (160°C fan-forced).

Toss the cubed root vegetables in the olive oil, place on a baking tray and season with salt. Roast for 40 minutes or until soft. Set aside to cool.

Bring a small saucepan of water to the boil, add the asparagus and blanch for 2–3 minutes. Drain and set aside to cool.

Combine the avocado, lettuce, carrot and tomato in a serving bowl. Add the asparagus and gently toss. Add the roasted vegetables and scatter on the sunflower seeds and feta, if desired, to finish.

Note

Make double the amount of roast vegetables and store them in an airtight container in the fridge. Add them to salads and sandwiches over the following days.

Lentil salad

SERVES 2

2 teaspoons olive oil
1 small zucchini, diced
1 cup canned brown lentils
¼ red onion, finely sliced
100 g cherry tomatoes, halved
80 g haloumi or feta cheese

Heat the olive oil in a frying pan over low heat, add the zucchini and cook for 5 minutes or until soft and golden on all sides.

Combine the lentils, onion and cherry tomatoes in a bowl. Add the zucchini and gently toss.

If using the haloumi, place the frying pan (no need to clean) over low heat, add the haloumi slices and cook for 5–10 minutes or until golden on each side. Add to the salad. If using the feta, simply crumble over the salad. Serve.

Chickpea salad

SERVES 2

1/2 avocado, sliced
1 cucumber, chopped
1/4 small red onion, sliced thinly
100 g cherry tomatoes, halved
1 cup canned chickpeas
60 g feta
1 teaspoon freshly squeezed lemon juice
1 teaspoon extra virgin olive oil

Combine the avocado, cucumber, onion and cherry tomatoes in a bowl. Add the chickpeas and gently stir.

Crumble the feta onto the salad, drizzle on the lemon juice and olive oil, toss and serve.

Note

Chickpeas are low-GI and high in fibre and protein, which helps you to feel fuller for longer. They also contain iron, folate and fatty acids.

Batch cooking and meal prepping

A great way to spend a weekend afternoon is to do some batch cooking for the week ahead, so that when witching hour kicks in, or you've had one of 'those' days, you can grab a healthy nourishing meal from your freezer. Batch cooking is excellent for your budget and meal planning, enabling you to get the most out of your weekly shop and reduce your food waste. Store your food in airtight containers or freezer bags, labelled with the date using a permanent marker or sticker to help you keep track of expiry. Frozen food is best kept for up to 3 months. When thawing, you can place the food in the fridge or use a microwave.

Crunchy noodle salad

SERVES 2

1 cup shredded lettuce
1 cup shredded red cabbage
½ avocado, sliced
1 carrot, chopped
1 tomato, chopped
½ cup crunchy noodles
¼ cup coarsely grated mozzarella

Dressing

2 tablespoons olive oil
1 tablespoon apple cider vinegar
1 teaspoon maple syrup

Place the lettuce, cabbage, avocado, carrot and tomato in a bowl and gently toss. Add the crunchy noodles and mozzarella.

Combine the dressing ingredients in a glass jar. Cover and shake to mix.

Pour the dressing over the salad and serve.

GRAB AND GO

There will always be times when you have to eat one-handed or on the run. It's handy to have some food options that contain some of the essential nutrients and vitamins that will help keep you feeling full while on the move.

- Greek yoghurt
- Chia pudding
- Edamame
- Cheese and crackers
- Nuts and seed mix
- Avocado on rice cake

Tempeh salad

SERVES 2

1 tablespoon olive oil
200 g tempeh, cut into 5 mm thick slices
¼ cup frozen corn kernels
Boiling water
1 cup shredded lettuce
100 g cherry tomatoes, halved
½ avocado, sliced
1 carrot, grated
½ cup canned chickpeas, drained
½ cup coarsely grated cheese (or vegan cheese)
1 tablespoon seed mix
1 tablespoon sesame seeds

Dressing

2 tablespoons olive oil
1 tablespoon hummus
2 tablespoons freshly squeezed lemon juice

Heat the olive oil in a frying pan over medium heat. Add the tempeh and cook for 4 minutes. Turn and cook for a further 4 minutes, or until evenly browned.

Place the corn in a heatproof bowl and cover with boiling water. Set aside to blanch for 5 minutes. Drain and set aside to cool.

Combine the dressing ingredients in a bowl and stir.

Place the lettuce, cherry tomatoes, avocado, carrot, chickpeas and corn in a bowl. Top with the cheese, drizzle on the dressing and gently toss. Sprinkle on the seed mix and sesame seeds and serve.

Oat biscuits

MAKES 12

½ cup peanut butter
2 tablespoons honey
1 tablespoon vanilla protein powder
1 cup rolled oats
2 tablespoons chia seeds

Preheat the oven to 200°C (180°C fan-forced). Line two baking trays with baking paper.

Place the peanut butter, honey and vanilla protein powder in a bowl and stir with a wooden spoon to mix well. Gently mix in the rolled oats and chia seeds.

Roll the dough into 12 balls, place on the trays and gently press to flatten slightly. Bake for 20 minutes or until golden on top.

Transfer the biscuits to a wire rack and allow to cool completely. Store in an airtight container.

Lactation chocolate chip biscuits

MAKES 12

60 g butter, melted
⅓ cup maple syrup
1 egg
1 tablespoon coconut oil or olive oil
1 teaspoon vanilla extract
1 cup (wholemeal or white) self-raising flour
4 tablespoons brewer's yeast
1/4 cup almond meal
1 teaspoon baking powder
2 cups rolled oats
1 cup chocolate chips

Preheat the oven to 200°C (180°C fan-forced). Line two baking trays with baking paper.

Place the melted butter, maple syrup, egg, coconut or olive oil and vanilla in a large bowl and mix well with electric beaters or a wooden spoon.

Sift in the flour, brewer's yeast and almond meal and mix until combined. Mix in the baking powder and rolled oats, then gently fold in the chocolate chips.

Roll the mixture into 12 balls, place on the trays and lightly press with a fork. Bake for 15–20 minutes or until golden brown.

Allow the biscuits to cool on the trays for 5 minutes, before transferring to a wire rack to cool completely. Store in an airtight container.

Healthy banana loaves

MAKES 6 LOAVES OR 12 MUFFINS

Coconut oil or butter, for greasing
1 egg
30 g butter, melted
1 teaspoon vanilla extract
1 tablespoon vanilla protein powder
⅓ cup pure maple syrup
3 bananas, mashed
1 ½ cups almond meal
¼ cup almond milk
60 g raisins

Preheat the oven to 200°C (180°C fan-forced).

Grease six mini loaf tins or a 12-hole muffin tray with coconut oil or butter.

Place the egg in a large bowl and lightly beat. Add the butter, vanilla extract, vanilla protein powder and maple syrup and stir with a spoon to combine.

Stir in the banana and raisins, then gently fold in the almond meal and almond milk.

Divide the batter evenly between the loaf tins or muffin tray and bake for 20 minutes or until the loaves or muffins are lightly golden on top. Cool in the tins or tray for 10 minutes, before transferring to a wire rack to cool completely.

Bliss balls

MAKES 12

Double the recipe and freeze half for future sweet cravings!

Chocolate bliss balls

½ cup chopped pitted medjool dates
1 teaspoon coconut oil
1½ tablespoons natural nut butter
1 teaspoon chai seeds
1 tablespoon vanilla protein powder
2 teaspoons cocoa powder
Shredded coconut, for rolling (optional)

Line a tray with baking paper. Place all the ingredients in a food processor or blender and whiz until finely crushed.

Take a tablespoon of the mixture and roll into a ball. Coat in the coconut, if desired, then place on the tray. Repeat until all the mixture has been used. Refrigerate for at least 1 hour before consuming. Store in the fridge in an airtight container.

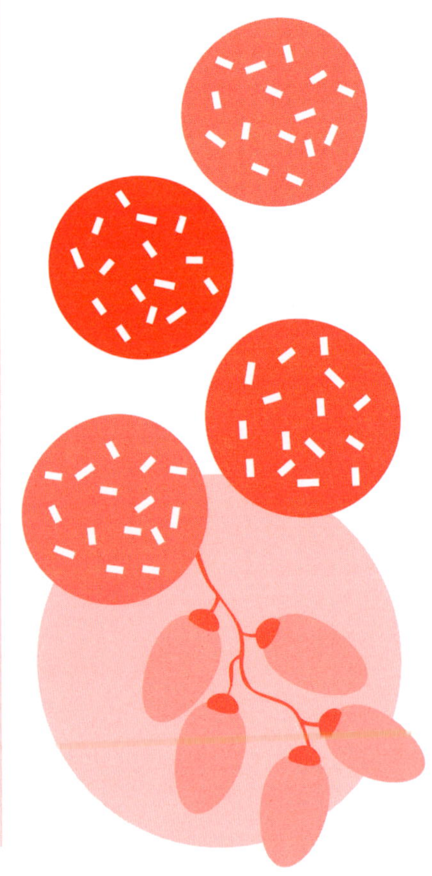

Lemon bliss balls

1 cup chopped pitted
  medjool dates
½ cup cashews
1 tablespoon almond meal
2 tablespoons chia seeds
1 teaspoon coconut oil
½ cup shredded coconut,
  plus extra for rolling
Grated zest of 1 lemon

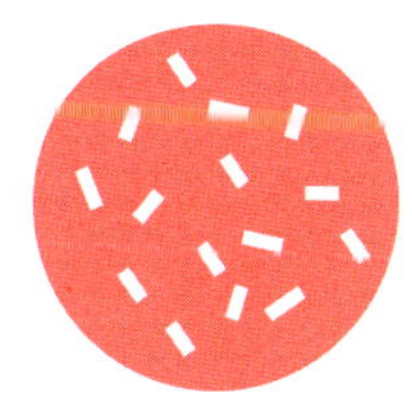

Line a tray with baking paper.

Place the dates, cashews, almond meal, chia seeds and coconut oil in a food processor or blender and whiz until a dough-like consistency. Add the zest and whiz for a further 1 minute.

Take a tablespoon of the mixture and roll into a ball. Coat in the shredded coconut, if desired, then place on the tray. Repeat until all the mixture has been used. Refrigerate for at least 1 hour before consuming. Store in the fridge in an airtight container.

Hydration

Good hydration is an essential part of overall health and nourishment. When you're dehydrated, your body cannot function properly. You may feel lethargic, struggle to regulate your body temperature and suffer from headaches. Hydration may also assist with healing, enhance your mood, improve sleep and support urinary issues that may arise after giving birth.

Breastfeeding mums require more water to stay hydrated as our bodies are working hard to produce breastmilk. In general, though, regardless of breastfeeding, staying hydrated is important but also something we forget when we are consumed by our babies and routines.

Have a drink bottle centrally located. Rather than reaching for drinks such as juice, soft drinks (including iced teas, which contain sugar), fill your drink bottle or glass with water and add lemon or mint to boost the flavour. You can also enjoy sparkling water to mix it up. Some mums like to have an alarm on their phone or watch to alert them to drink and keep up water intake.

When you visit the bathroom, check how hydrated you are by noting the colour of your urine. When you're dehydrated, it will be yellow or a dark shade of yellow, due to your body retaining as much fluid as possible. If your urine is a pale yellow or clear, this is a good sign that you are well hydrated.

CAFFEINE

You're probably waking after a long, sleepless night and looking forward to holding that warm cup of coffee in the morning, as you steady yourself for another day. You might be like so many mums who attempt to drink a number of coffees in the day, half-finished and mostly cold!

Caffeine in coffee is a stimulant, which means it may give you symptoms such as the jitters, heart palpitations, dehydration, anxiety and irritability, dizziness and restlessness. If you're a coffee drinker, aim to drink it in the morning before 11 am to ensure you maintain your natural circadian rhythms of a regular wake/sleep cycle, particularly when you're waking frequently to feed your baby.

If you are breastfeeding, a small amount of caffeine is thought to pass through breastmilk and can subsequently affect your baby in a similar way it affects you. If you really can't live without it, you might look at replacing your second or third coffee with a decaf option.

Coffee is a necessary part of my self-care routine. I love the smell that fills my house in the mornings and I love sitting holding the warm cup in my hands while I chat with my husband and kids.

My biggest tip – one I learnt very early on in motherhood – is to always drink my coffee from a cup with a lid. The unpredictability of parenthood may mean a nappy change or a nap is imminent, so I always have that KeepCup handy!

ALCOHOL

Having a glass of wine might be a form of self-care for you. For many people, this is a 'treat'. We all have our guilty pleasures such as chocolate, wine, coffee or sweets and, in moderation, that is okay. It is, however, recommended that the safest option for breastfeeding mothers is to not consume alcohol.

If there is a special occasion and you're still breastfeeding, there are a few ways in which you can enjoy a drink, and this includes planning ahead. Alcohol can stay in your system for up to 2 hours for one standard drink. This means that you will need to allow time after consuming alcohol, and you may need to supplement your baby's feeds with pumped breastmilk or formula in a bottle.

The truth about pump and dump

Pump and dump is the term used to describe expressing breastmilk to reduce the alcohol levels within breastmilk and throwing it away. The Australian Breastfeeding Association does not recommend doing this, as it does not actually reduce the amount of alcohol in your breastmilk. You may choose to pump and dump as a way to relieve breast engorgement, however.

As it takes 2 hours per standard drink to rid the alcohol from your breastmilk, you'll need to think ahead. For example, if you are planning to have a few drinks at an event, you may choose to express in advance to feed your baby and then pump and dump for comfort reasons before resuming breastfeeding after enough time has passed for the alcohol to leave your body.

You are strong and capable. You are doing the best you can.

PART 2

Emotional self-care

Mental health

Emotional self-care can tend to take a backseat when we become parents. Parenting is such an incredible experience and is filled with so much excitement and love, but can also be incredibly stressful and challenging at times. We face many challenges, both anticipated and unexpected. Self-care gives us the strength to face these, and reminds us to be kind to ourselves, celebrate the little wins when they come and, when things feel overwhelming, use our self-care rituals.

Practising self-care can nurture your mental wellbeing and build your resilience, which may help you to better manage the emotional moments and hurdles we all experience.

Our minds require nourishment too.

Parenthood can feel like the never-ending rotation of responsibilities, and it can wear us down when we don't make the space and time to pause, engage in our own self-care and reflect on what we're grateful for.

The brain, just like any organ in the body, needs nourishment. Just as we look after ourselves when we get the flu, our mental health requires care too.

Hormones such as dopamine, serotonin and oxytocin play a key role in maintaining mental health. Engaging in self-help activities can help to boost those hormones that make us feel good.

However, it's important to note that you may need additional support for mental health issues including panic disorder and depression. Reach out to your GP, who will put you in touch with a mental health professional.

SEROTONIN

Serotonin, which plays a key role in regulating our mood and in our overall mental health, can be found in the brain and the digestive tract. Here are some ways to boost your serotonin levels.

- Exercise regularly in any form for 20–30 minutes a day.
- Practise meditation and mindfulness.
- Vitamin D exposure – get out in the sunshine for 10–30 minutes a day, before 11 am or after 4 pm.
- Eat a healthy diet that is rich in tryptophan, an essential amino acid, as well as omega 3 and omega 6 fatty acids and B vitamins. Include fish (predominantly salmon), eggs, cheese, spinach and nuts and seeds in your diet.

ENDORPHINS

Neurotransmitters made by the pituitary gland and the central nervous system, endorphins assist with reducing pain and stress. You've probably heard about their association with exercise. The following ideas are all endorphin-boosters.

- Take a warm bath.
- Acupuncture.
- Watch a comedy or laugh with a friend.
- Indulge in dark chocolate or a glass of wine.
- Swim in the ocean.
- Exercise.

OXYTOCIN

Known as the 'love hormone', oxytocin affects our physical and psychological wellbeing, including reducing stress responses in the brain. It plays a role in enhancing those contractions to bring your baby through the birth canal and into the world and it is the hormone that is released when you're breastfeeding. Here are ways to promote oxytocin naturally.

- Have sex.
- Hug and kiss your family.
- Practise yoga.
- Listen to music.
- Get a massage.

You
are more
capable
than you
know
or
realise.

Skin-to-skin

Skin-to-skin contact with your baby is a lovely way to relax and be present in the moment. Take the time to pause and let it be an opportunity to practise mindfulness. Usually done immediately after giving birth, regular skin-to-skin contact can be continued for as long as you like, as often as you like. It encourages breastfeeding by increasing your production of prolactin and oxytocin, the feel-good hormones that are important for the letdown reflex. But you don't need to be breastfeeding to enjoy some calming skin-to-skin time with your baby.

Relax into this perfect window of time.

Skin-to-skin reduces the cortisol levels in both you and your baby, and promotes bonding. Beneficial for regulating your baby's temperature, heart rate and respiratory rates, it can reduce your baby's frequency of crying. It is a beautiful time to bond, and a perfect window of time to really enjoy the moment, all while promoting your own wellbeing, as well as your baby's, through connection and love.

Baby blues

Seventy-five per cent of women experience the baby blues, which tend to present themselves around three to five days after giving birth. When a woman experiences the baby blues, she tends to feel emotional, moody, teary, anxious or overwhelmed. It is not a mental health condition, but it can last up to two weeks. Many hormonal changes occur at this time, including when your milk comes in.

Many factors can contribute to the baby blues, including:

- hormonal changes
- sleep deprivation
- learning and navigating a new role
- the healing process post-birth, which can make us feel a little more fragile.

If you are feeling hopeless or experiencing panic attacks or thoughts of harming yourself, you need to seek support from a professional. Find someone you feel safe and comfortable talking to – this can be your midwife, your doctor/GP or a psychologist.

At times, we all need to reach out for support, and that is okay. You don't have to do it alone. Try to not minimise your emotions. Your feelings, no matter how big or small, are always valid.

I found that asking for help from those closest to me sometimes led to disappointment when I wasn't emotionally supported the way I needed to be in that moment. I discovered that reaching for support from someone not as close to the situation was more beneficial for me, so I sought help from cousins, friends and my GP. Sometimes, the best support can come from unexpected sources. Reaching out to others can make a profound difference to your life.

Your partner

Your partner can also experience depression and anxiety before or after the birth. It is important that they take care of themselves during the postpartum period, as they learn to find their feet and deal with the emotional and physical changes. Encourage your partner to speak to a health professional or reach out to a support group if you notice any signs of depression or anxiety.

Your feelings are always valid.

WHEN YOUR BABY CRIES

It can be difficult to hear your baby cry, particularly when we are used to being in control in many other facets of our lives, or we aren't quite sure what is wrong and what the baby needs. You might feel overwhelmed, distressed or upset; it might feel like your baby will never stop crying. But it doesn't mean you're doing anything wrong.

Here are some ways to keep yourself calm when your baby cries:

- **Skin-to-skin with your baby (see page 127) is proven to assist with calming and soothing babies, and can help to regulate your own heart rate.**
- **Breathe, taking deep, long breaths in and out.**
- **Practise self-kindness and remind yourself that you are doing the best you can, that all babies cry and that this too will pass.**
- **Ask your partner to stay with the baby while you step outside – taking turns will give you both the chance to feel calmer.**
- **Sing or play soft music.**
- **Wear your baby using a carrier or sling (although if you are feeling exhausted or stressed, you may find using the pram to soothe your baby to sleep is a better option).**

You are
seen
and you are
appreciated,
even if it
doesn't quite
feel like it
today.

Perinatal depression and anxiety

Perinatal is inclusive of conception, during pregnancy and up to 24 months after birth.

Risk factors, such as a history of depression and anxiety or having experienced perinatal mental health issues in a previous pregnancy, can play a part in developing perinatal depression and anxiety. Factors that can have an effect include:

- **if the pregnancy was unplanned, or unwanted**
- **feeling ambivalent during the pregnancy**
- **having limited social support around you**
- **experiencing issues with breastfeeding**
- **experiencing complications in labour and birth, birth trauma or Post Traumatic Stress Disorder.**

What isn't commonly talked about is the complications that arise in pregnancy, labour and birth that may cause birth trauma (see opposite) and affect the way a woman is feeling emotionally when she enters the space of motherhood.

DID YOU KNOW?

One in seven women will experience perinatal depression and one in five will experience perinatal anxiety. One in ten dads will experience postnatal depression and anxiety.

Birth trauma

Birth doesn't always go to plan. Birth trauma may present in a physical and/or psychological form. The reasons for birth trauma are varied but can include a prolonged labour, an emergency situation (such as an emergency caesarean), labour and birth that didn't go as planned, complications for mother and/or baby, or if labour or birth were triggers for past experiences such as late-term pregnancy loss.

Birth trauma is diagnosed by a qualified clinical psychologist or psychiatrist and may come under the banner of PTSD.

If you are experiencing symptoms such as anxiety, aggressive behaviour, low mood, depression, feelings of hopelessness, or triggering events (including places, people, smells, nightmares or repetitive recollections), or any combination of the above, there is help available to you. Reach out to a health professional for support.

Signs and symptoms of perinatal anxiety and depression include:

- feeling sad or experiencing low mood
- crying often
- persistent worrying
- irritation or frustration
- physical symptoms, such as trembling hands, heart palpitations, nausea and vomiting
- changes in appetite
- difficulty sleeping or sleeping too much
- being unable to find the joy in things that you used to
- having panic attacks
- experiencing thoughts of harming yourself
- withdrawing from family and friends
- fear of being alone with your baby
- feeling isolated or unsure where to go.

If you are experiencing any symptoms of perinatal anxiety and depression, know that there is lots of support available and that reaching out is not a sign of weakness, but a sign of strength. It can be frightening to experience these symptoms, especially if you feel pressure to be overjoyed with your new arrival. But feeling this way and talking to someone about it doesn't make you less loving or capable as a mother, and you should not suffer in silence.

Navigating your new role can be daunting, and sometimes even disappointing, and all mothers experience different emotions that are associated with this new change in their lives. Similarly, motherhood can open up old wounds or past experiences, for example if you had a difficult relationship with a parent, or have experienced bereavement.

The good news is that perinatal anxiety and depression is treatable. A health professional can support you in a non-judgemental way, and give you the tools and care that you need.

Perinatal anxiety and depression are treatable.

It is okay to not feel okay.

How to look after your mental health

- Talk to someone that you trust. Be open and honest about how you're feeling and communicate what you need. It is okay to admit you're not enjoying certain aspects of motherhood.

- Be kind to yourself. Focus on connection with yourself and your family during this time; it isn't selfish to look after yourself.

- Say no. This might give you the freedom to check in with what you need right now and what is best for your mental wellbeing.

- Take time. Take a moment. Recalibrate.

- Know that you are not alone.

Q&A
WITH PSYCHOLOGIST **DR SARAH HUGHES**

Dr Sarah Hughes is a mother, clinical psychologist and author.

Is it normal to find motherhood challenging and difficult at times?

Yes, it is hard and can be challenging at times for all parents, particularly new parents. It is important to recognise that it isn't going to be perfect and that some days you may think to yourself that you are not enjoying the experience. Many mothers feel this way and it can take time to find your feet in your new role.

How do I find time for myself when I am feeling burnt out?

Aim to find pockets of time to do something that feels right for you. Start with small bursts. This might be a 20-minute run instead of your usual hour that you did pre-kids. Not only will you feel better for it, but it can give you that much-needed energy. Finding 15–20 minutes a few times a week might be all that's possible right now for you and that's okay.

Is it common to feel guilt around leaving my baby or taking time out for myself?

Guilt can be very common for both parents. The best thing you can do for your child is to do the best thing for you. Self-care might be working two days a week and putting your child into care or having a family member mind them.

I have been feeling low for a few weeks now and not enjoying my motherhood experience. I cannot seem to find joy in the things I used to do. What should I do?

Firstly, know that there is support and that you are not alone. The best place to start is opening up and talking to someone you trust. That may be your partner, a family member or friend.

Booking an appointment with your GP is also a good first step. You can discuss your feelings, and they can write you a care plan, including putting you in touch with a psychologist.

It can be hard for parents to access psychologists, due to location, limited care for your child, etc. If this is the case, you can ask to make a telehealth appointment, which can be beneficial when baby is very young too.

When you're feeling in a slump, your baby is having a developmental leap or you've been at home with your little one all day, you might like to give yourself a little bit of love.

These are some simple way to fill up your cup.

- **Have a cup of tea and arrange a chat with a friend.**
- **Order healthy takeaway for dinner, or pull out a frozen meal.**
- **Enjoy some uninterrupted reading time, even if it is only 10 minutes.**
- **Get out for a walk in the sunshine.**
- **Put on some relaxing music.**
- **Get your partner to give you a foot massage or take a bath.**
- **Stimulate your vagus nerve by breathing slowly and doing deep belly breaths.**

Self-compassion

Taking the time for self-compassion doesn't mean you're selfish or egotistical. Being kind to ourselves can prevent burnout and helps us to identify effective ways to cope when we are feeling overwhelmed.

We are often way too hard on ourselves. You need to remember how far you have come and everything you have achieved. This is the time to love yourself. You have grown a human being inside you. You have nourished your baby, grown a placenta and given birth. Your body has gone through changes both physiologically and emotionally and you are now nuturing and loving your baby.

This is the time to love yourself.

Be kind to yourself and allow yourself to ride the waves of motherhood, its ebbs and its flows. Make taking care of you a priority and reward yourself from time to time. This might be having a coffee with a friend, buying yourself a new novel or going to a yoga class on your own.

We can be our harshest critic. Try your best to avoid self-judgement. Don't buy into notion of needing to be busy all the time when you have a new baby. Allow yourself to let go of expectations. You don't need to have a tidy house, cook everything from scratch or exercise every day!

Love yourself a little more

- Acknowledge your feelings.
- Celebrate the small wins.
- Avoid negative self-talk.
- Do something you love.
- Remind yourself that you are enough and that you are worthy.

Feeling overwhelmed?

There is no escaping that some days are a struggle. Self-compassion is so beneficial in building resilience and self-confidence at this time. When you're feeling overwhelmed, take a few deep breaths and ask yourself, *What can I do in this moment to reduce the overwhelm?*

For example, your baby may not be taking a bottle or latching onto the breast and you are feeling upset and frustrated. The resolution may be taking your baby outside for a moment, calming them, calming yourself and trying again, or asking your partner or a family member to help if possible.

In this moment, it's important to accept that you are trying your best but everything new takes time and practice. Go easy on yourself and know you are learning every single day.

Our babies depend on us. Their needs can consume our minds, bodies and emotions. When you have more than one child, you can feel pulled in different directions. There will be days when energy is low, when just getting up, taking a shower and making the bed feels like it's too much. You are beyond tired and your third cup of coffee isn't cutting it.

We all have days like these; motherhood is hard and challenges us.

These are exactly the times when you need to nurture your self-compassion the most. You are not perfect but you are enough. You are worthy, and taking a step back to take some time for yourself doesn't change that. In fact, it helps you to look after others.

When you're overwhelmed, ask yourself:

- **Is my baby loved?**
- **Is my baby safe?**
- **Is my baby cared for?**
- **Is my baby fed and warm?**

If the answer is yes, then you are doing an incredible job!

What can I do in this moment?

- **Take deep breaths using the square breathing technique (see page 160).**
- **Give yourself a hand massage.**
- **Be gentle with yourself when you make a mistake – catch that negative self-talk in the moment and quash it.**

We all have imperfections and we don't get everything right a hundred per cent of the time. This is the perfect space to show yourself compassion and remind yourself that you are doing an incredible job.

Change the way you speak to yourself

Making some simple changes to your self-talk can make such a difference, especially in the early days when there is so much to learn. Adjust your language to be kind and compassionate and give yourself grace to find your way.

- Swap 'I have to . . .' to 'I can . . .' For example, 'I can wake up and shower.'
- Celebrate how far you've come in getting to know your baby. For example, 'I've learnt that my baby likes to be burped before lying flat in the bassinet.'
- Mantras can help you to be present, reflect and think positively. Try: 'Today is a new day.'
- When times are tough, say to yourself: 'This feels very hard right now, but I am managing the best I can.'
- It can be frustrating when your baby is at certain developmental points. Instead of saying, 'I cannot wait for them to . . . !', try saying 'I'm looking forward to when they . . . !'
- Talk to yourself as you would talk to a friend.

What does self-compassion look like?

- Saying no and being okay with it.
- Deleting an app or social media that is not serving you right now.
- Cutting your to-do list.
- Taking a break from the news.
- Looking after your body.
- Doing things in your own time.

I don't think there is a mum who hasn't experienced guilt at some point in their parenting journey.

It doesn't matter what you do, you'll have moments of feeling guilty. It comes with the job, right? You may at times question yourself and whether you are doing things the 'right' way. In fact, questioning your decisions only shows that you care deeply about your baby and want the best for them.

Guilt can steal too much of your life, if you let it. Self-kindness is something I have struggled with since becoming a mum of two. For me, it was the guilt that really stopped me from making the time for myself.

Honour what you have achieved.

Every day, I try to combat that inner voice and be more conscious of what I say to myself. It is an ongoing journey.

Try these tips to build your self-compassion.

- **In this moment, honour what you've achieved so far.**
- **Don't compare yourself to others: we are all on our own journey and our babies are all different.**
- **It is okay to outgrow places and people.**
- **Tell yourself something kind, something you would say to a friend experiencing what you are experiencing right now.**

Creating boundaries

Sometimes self-care isn't about engaging in leisure activities. It may be about creating boundaries or making decisions, such as saying no. If you've recently returned to work after maternity leave, boundaries may look like not answering emails, working out of work hours when you get home or when you're with your baby, reducing your hours, reducing the number of night shifts you do (if you're a shift worker) and being open and honest about workloads or concerns with your manager when they arise. Or your boundaries may involve saying no to visits from family and friends, and instead spending time together as your new family unit. Show yourself compassion and make space for what you need right now.

Let go of perfectionism, judgement and self-doubt.

Q&A

WITH PSYCHOLOGIST **DR REBECCA RAY**

Dr Rebecca Ray is a clinical psychologist, author and speaker.

How is self-kindness important in mothering?

Motherhood is life-altering. Please honour the process of adjustment by beginning your motherhood journey in a protective bubble that you imagine around yourself, free from judgement and comparison. Give yourself the time and space to navigate this new life and the new dynamic with the little life you created. Make the time to find your own way without taking on the background noise of others' opinions and allowing them to influence who you are becoming as a new parent. Self-kindness is particularly beneficial if the transition into motherhood has been challenging, or it takes some time to connect with your baby. We walk our own paths and have our own experiences to arrive in motherhood.

So, what is self-kindness?

Self-kindness is when you are essentially holding your own hand. It is about speaking to yourself with compassion and respect. An easy way to begin to apply self-kindness is through speaking to yourself like you would a friend. What would you say to a friend that was going through this? What would you say to a friend who is struggling in this moment? Our identity changes with motherhood and it can take time to completely step into that role. Embrace it. Reject the urge to look outside yourself to check that you are doing it 'right' and instead, return to your intuition. Self-kindness is the process of nurturing your relationship with the most important person on this journey: you. Because baby thrives when you are gentle on yourself.

Can I apply self-kindness in other ways?

Yes! Start by surrounding yourself with emotionally safe people. People who speak to you respectfully, who care for your well-being, and who you can trust to hold non-judgemental space for you to simply be as you are right now. Next, make choices that feel aligned for you rather than trying to be someone you are not, or someone you think you 'should' be. And finally, we all have moments as mothers when we are deeply vulnerable and emotionally fragile.

In these times, choose self-forgiveness and remember that you are doing the best you can with you know and have.

Some final tips:

- Set boundaries and make your own choices, for example, choosing to opt out of mothers' groups. Just because it's a great fit for your antenatal class friend doesn't mean you'll love it, too. Try it on and see what fits for you and your baby.
- Unsubscribe, unfollow, mute, and step back from things that don't serve you to be the person you want to be during this chapter.
- Give yourself permission to mother the way you want to.
- Replenish your energy and take time to rest, especially in honouring the energy you have available on any given day. You can't do all the things, but you can do a few things in a very aligned way.

TRIGGERS

You may identify there are certain things that 'trigger' an emotional response or increase that feeling of fight-or-flight in your body. It is normal for us as human beings to have emotional responses to certain situations, events, or circumstances. Learning how to identify your triggers may lead to a better understanding and a strategy to cope with them when they occur, and managing the symptoms that show up in your body.

You may not notice that you have triggers until you have a baby, or maybe there are external factors such as sleep deprivation that make can make us feel more irritable and sensitive. It is important to recognise that if you are experiencing this fight-or-flight response on a regular basis, or it is affecting your ability to do everyday tasks, then it may be a good time to reach out and speak with a trusted health professional.

Triggers include:

- noise, such as when your baby cries
- constant touch
- sleep deprivation
- going out in public, especially in the early days.

Little reminders

- ○ You are learning and growing.
- ○ Saying no to something that doesn't feel right is okay.
- ○ No one is perfect.
- ○ We all have weaknesses.
- ○ You are doing an incredible job.

Mindfulness

Mindfulness is the act of bringing your awareness to the present moment, focusing on how you are feeling within your mind as well as any sensations within your body. Mindfulness encourages us to live in the present and focus on the moment in a neutral way.

Mindfulness may reduce your stress levels, improve your sleep, increase your energy levels and boost your overall mental health and wellbeing. It is particularly useful for parents, allowing you to bring your awareness back to how you are feeling and to calm your thoughts before reacting in situations. After birth, everything becomes more heightened, as now we have not only ourselves to think about but a new baby too.

When you practise mindfulness, you can allow thoughts to come in and out of your mind, but not buy into them. When a thought arises, recognise it, then let it go. Visualise it flowing down a river. You can learn to accept your current situation or what you're experiencing in the moment without judging or being harsh on yourself. Listen to yourself and your body. Take note of any physical symptoms, and consider where your mind wanders to and what your thoughts are telling you.

Engaging in mindfulness is an art that needs to be practised and it takes time to learn. By focusing on the present moment and using mindfulness techniques, you can adapt when emotions feel overwhelming and learn to soothe yourself in difficult or challenging situations.

Ways to practise mindfulness

- Slow down and take some deep breaths, focusing on your breath as you exhale and inhale. Be present in the moment.
- Practise yoga or stretching.
- Meditate.
- Listen to music that is soothing or relaxing.
- Go for a walk in nature.

Creating a mindfulness space

Choose a dedicated space that is not cluttered or messy, away from the dishes or the laundry pile. This can help you to focus on yourself and how you are feeling, rather than what needs to be tended to. This space can be a chair in the bedroom or outside; it just needs to be somewhere you can get comfortable and allow yourself a little bit of time to clear your mind, slow your thoughts and breathe deeply.

When you are creating your space, consider lighting, noise, music and a blanket or pillow for warmth. Mindfulness for you may be simply taking time alone to sit in silence with a cup of tea, or even taking a short nap.

Be present in the moment

We hear this phrase a lot, but what does it actually mean? Being present in the moment is a way to self-soothe. By being present, you become aware of your senses (smell, taste, sight, touch, sound) and it's a great way to work on gratitude (see page 164), particularly with a new baby. An easy way to do this is to focus on your baby, their skin, smell, face, hair. What are they doing? How are they breathing? Then refocus to yourself and how you are feeling. How is your body positioned? What do you feel like in this moment? Breathe.

Body scan

A body scan is a way to focus on how each part of your body is feeling. You look for sensations, movements in your limbs, your heartbeat and any tightness in your muscles, working your way from one end of your body to another.

If you have ever taken a yoga class, you may be aware of the body scan. This is something I regularly do when lying on the lounge or in bed. It is so simple yet so effective. If you are new to it and prefer to have a guided body scan, there are plenty online that will help you through.

I like to start at my head and work my way down my body.

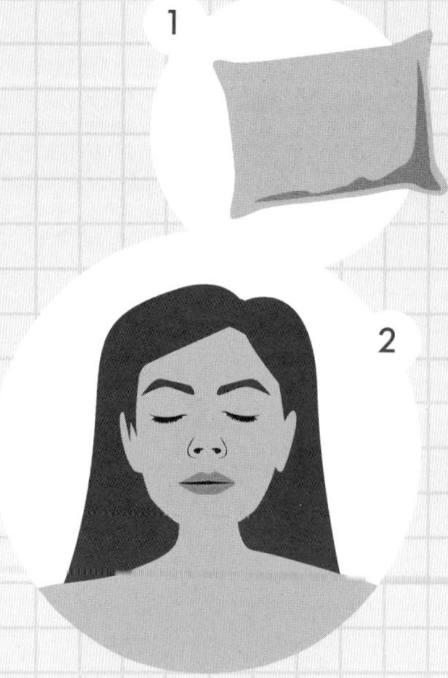

1. Get comfortable and aim to be lying flat.

2. Think about your head, your ears, your jaw – bring your awareness to how they feel. Does it feel tight in your jaw? Is your face relaxed? Move to your neck and shoulders and take a few breaths, letting go of any tension. You can do this by squeezing, holding for one second and relaxing, or simply focus on relaxing the area by letting the parts of the body become heavy.

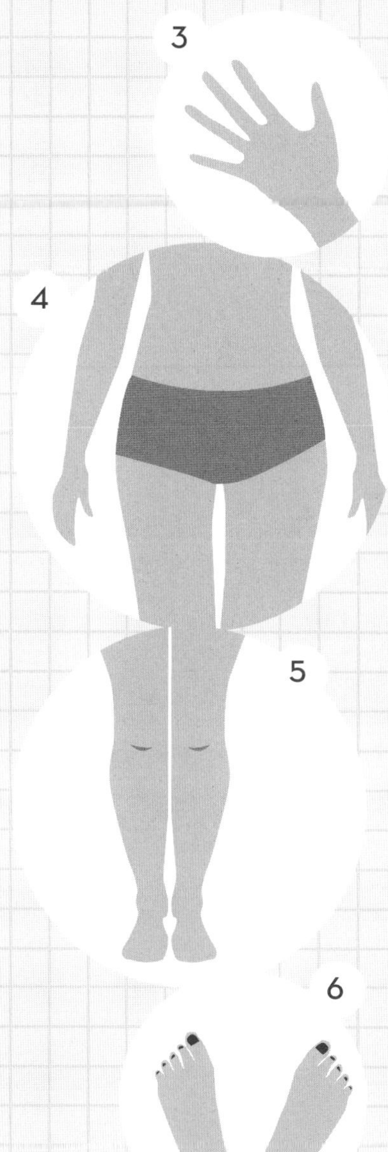

3. Focus on your arms, your fingers. Consciously thinking about each finger and your palms. Take a few breaths, releasing any tension.

4. Move down your body and repeat on each part: your stomach, your back, lower back, hips and buttocks. Let go of any tension you are feeling. Take a few breaths, releasing any tension.

5. Then focus on your thighs, outer thighs, knees, legs. Do they feel sore? Are you able to relax them? Take a few breaths, releasing any tension.

6. Allow your feet to fall to the side. Then move down to your feet and ankles. Take a few breaths, releasing any tension.

After some practice, you'll find your own best way of moving through the body scan and re-laxing further with each breath, ensuring that when your mind wanders, you bring it back to the focus on the breath.

SQUARE BREATHING TECHNIQUE

The square breathing technique is a way to focus on your breathing and to slow it down by stimulating the vagus nerve, which is responsible for regulating your heart rate and respiratory rate and stabilising activity within the brain. This is a simple and easy-to-use technique – a good one for in the car when your baby is crying and you can feel your heart rate increasing, or when your emotions are overwhelming and you're experiencing an anxious tightening of the chest. Listen to yourself and your body.

Start at the top left corner and move clockwise.

- **Breathe in for 1, 2, 3, 4 (along the top of the square).**
- **Hold for 1, 2, 3, 4 (down the right side of the square).**
- **Breathe out for 1, 2, 3, 4 (along the bottom of the square) .**
- **Hold for 1, 2, 3, 4 up the left side.**

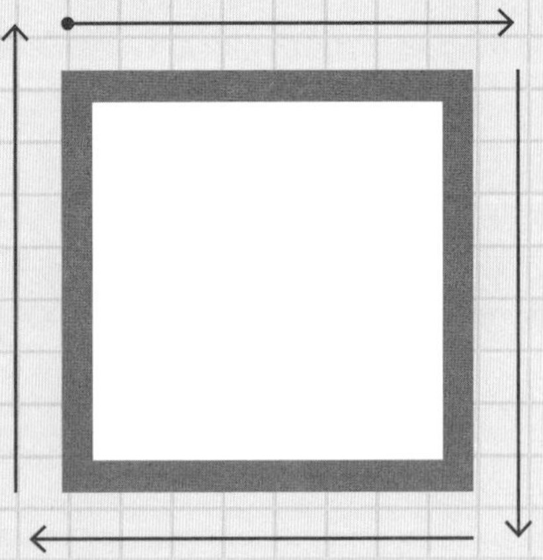

VISUALISATION

Visualisation is a great form of mindfulness that you can do anywhere at any time.

Take a seat, close your eyes and visualise a happy memory: someone you love, a song or something you're looking forward to. Let your mind wander to this place and think about how you were feeling in the moment and what was special about it. Tell yourself that little story.

APPS FOR MINDFULNESS

- **Calm** - meditation app that is useful for sleep and guided meditation.
- **Smiling Mind** - meditation app developed by psychologists.
- **Headspace** - mindfulness app for meditation and mindfulness activities for stress, sleep, anxiety and sleep.
- **Calming music** on YouTube or Spotify.

Affirmations

Affirmations are a great way to encourage positive thinking.

Positive thinking doesn't always come naturally. Using affirmations regularly can encourage new neural pathways in the brain to form, essentially training our brains to think in a positive way by forming the habit. This in turn leads to a boost in self-confidence and self-kindness.

Affirmations may be helpful as a new mum, when you are constantly learning new things and navigating a different way of life. It's about reminding yourself regularly of all the wonderful things you are doing and going gently when things go wrong.

Affirmations: Week 1

- My feelings matter.
- I am doing the best I can in this present moment.
- It's okay not to have the answers.

Affirmations: Week 2

- I am proud of how far I have come.
- I am in charge of how I feel and today I choose happiness.
- I am growing through every experience.

Affirmations: Week 3

- I am growing, learning and discovering myself and my baby in this new role.
- I am stronger than I think.
- I will celebrate my small wins.

Affirmations: Week 4

- I trust in my decisions of what is best for me and my baby.
- This is tough but so am I.
- I am doing my best.
- I am worthy.

Gratitude

Gratitude can help us to see the positive in situations and encourage us to build a strong relationship with ourselves.

A gratitude journal is a great way of training our minds to think optimistically, as this doesn't always come naturally, particularly when things are challenging or we are going through a period of change.

This was instrumental in helping me change my mindset and allowing me to see the positives in my life when I was feeling anxious or overwhelmed.

Research has shown that writing in a gratitude journal can increase our happiness levels. This doesn't mean you need to write every day or for long periods of time. Start small. It may be writing in the evenings before you go to sleep or first thing when you wake up, and simply jotting down three things that you are grateful for.

You might do this a few times a week or it may become part of your daily routine.

Be proud of what you have achieved. Reflect on how far you have come as well as the journey you have taken to get to this point.

If gratitude journalling is not your thing, or you are pressed for time, try writing down your intentions. You might do this for the day or the week, or note how you can be kinder to yourself. Sometimes it is just about planting that seed in your mind.

Journal prompts

What are three things you are good at?

What are your three strongest qualities?

What are you most grateful for?

What do you love most about being a parent?

What makes you happy?

What are you feeling worried about at this present time?

Asking for help

Asking for help can be difficult, particularly if you are not used to it or don't know where to start. You may not know how to ask for it, or you might feel guilty or embarrassed seeking help as a new mother.

Motherhood is incredibly rewarding. It is also a more than full-time job, and it can undoubtably be stressful. When experiencing perinatal depression and anxiety, it can alter your capacity to care for your own needs and your baby's needs.

Never ignore your mental health; prioritise it. It can take time to find your feet in your new role as a mother, and recognising that you aren't feeling good is the first step in seeking help.

Parenthood takes time to adjust to. It can be normal to feel overwhelmed, emotional and frustrated with the changes, especially with the hormone shifts after giving birth. It is important to recognise that it is okay to not enjoy motherhood 24/7. What isn't normal is when we feel sad, anxious or worried consistently and these feelings take over from the enjoyment of daily life.

You are not alone. Help is here.

Your doctor

GPs are great at supporting you with the necessary information about local psychology services. They can also do a mental health care plan, which enables you to get Medicare funding to assist in the costs of seeing a psychologist.

Your midwife or child and family health nurse

Speak with your midwife or child and family health nurse at your next appointment, or reach out to the women's care unit at your local hospital or community health centre.

A psychologist

Look for a psychologist you feel you can trust and who makes you feel comfortable.

Lifeline 13 11 14

A 24-hour telephone crisis support service for anyone needing mental or emotional support.

The Gidget Foundation

This foundation has support centres, telehealth or virtual appointments as well as other programs depending on your needs. You can contact them 24/7 through their app, Gidget Perinatal Support Centre.

Perinatal Anxiety & Depression Australia

PANDA supports mothers and families affected by depression and anxiety during pregnancy and in the first year after birth. For more information, go to panda.org.au.

Beyond Blue

Provides mental health information and support for anyone in Australia. Find more information at beyondblue.org.au.

See the Resources section on page 200 for more support services and their contact details.

PART 3

Social self-care

Your relationship

Communication is key in any relationship. When it comes to self-care, communicating your needs is essential. Set time aside for a conversation with your partner, in which you can discuss, listenand explore ways to incorporate self-care, both individually and as a couple.

It can be easy to neglect this when we are wrapped up in our responsibilities, but it will give both of you a much-needed boost and moment to pause. So, for example, you might decide to set aside Sunday for self-care: you have time to yourself in the morning and then swap with your partner at lunchtime so they can take a break. Or you may designate a weekday evening for an exercise class, team sport or seeing a friend. Mix it up in a way that works for you.

Try to set regular time aside as a couple too, even if it is a monthly date night at home. Lean on friends or family to achieve this. You'll be surprised how much people love to help and enjoy being able to support you (and spend time with your baby!).

Remember that you and your partner are a team. There is no guidebook, particularly in the early days, when you are learning so much about yourself, your baby and each other. The demands of parenthood can be exhausting and put pressure on your relationship. Keep lines of communication open. Let your partner know when you need to take a step back and encourage them to be open with you. Making time for self-care will allow you both to be better partners and parents.

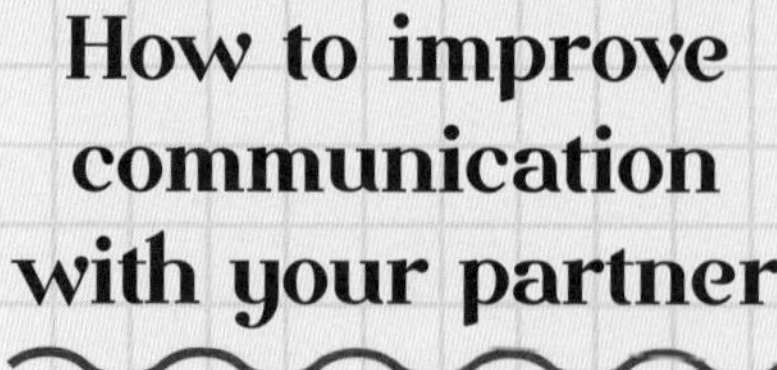

How to improve communication with your partner

- Make an effort to speak kindly to each other, even when you are sleep-deprived and irritable.
- Be patient with one another – you're both learning!
- Listen to and acknowledge each other's opinions and suggestions.
- Give your partner the space to find their own way of doing things, even if it is different to yours.
- Work as a team. Take turns settling, bathing and/or feeding your baby.
- Allow yourself to be vulnerable with each other. Foster honesty and openness.

- Encourage each other to take self-care time. Doing something you love or that makes you happy will renew your energy and in turn help you to become a better partner and parent.

- Allow your partner to take the lead and trust in their ability. We can get swamped by our mothering role and innately take the lead, but when we step back and allow our partners and family members to be involved it lightens our load and allows them to establish that caring and bonding role too.

Date ideas for new parents

- Cook a simple dinner together after you've put your baby to sleep.
- Listen to a playlist of songs that mean something to you as a couple. Enjoy the memories they evoke.
- Order in takeaway and watch a movie.
- Connect through touch. This doesn't need to be sexual. It could be a foot massage, or curling up together on the sofa.
- Lighten the mood by watching your favourite comedy show.
- Play a game of cards or a boardgame.
- Call on your support people to look after your baby while you spend some one-on-one time together. You might grab some lunch or an early dinner, go for a walk or just do the shopping together.

Parental burnout

Some days, we think we have it all together: we juggle the sleep schedule, feeding, housework, work, exercise and our relationships. Other days, nothing goes to plan.

All parents experience this. You are not alone. The trouble is that because we are juggling so much, we can often miss the signs of parental burnout, including:

- exhaustion
- feelings of persistent guilt
- lack of motivation
- increased anxiety
- feeling overwhelmed
- not enjoying the moments of parenthood.

I don't think there is a parent out there that hasn't experienced some sort of parental burnout. It may be to do with balancing work and home life. Maybe it's just you haven't been able to incorporate self-care into your life for what feels like months and you need a little break. Other things that can lead to burnout include:

- always striving or comparing
- focusing on the negatives rather than the positives
- not making the time to eat well, rest and move your body
- not getting enough sleep
- not making time for activities you enjoy or spending time with friends
- trying to please everyone
- trying to control everything (this is difficult with babies, who can be unpredictable)
- feeling guilty when having some time for self-care.

Recharging when you can, even in short bursts, will help you to build up reserves and prevent burnout. Try not to be hard on yourself, and keep connected to those around you, whether that's family or friends or your partner.

Know that it is okay to ask for help – in fact it is the best thing to do for you and your baby.

Tips for when you're experiencing burnout

- Reach for your self-care tool kit (see page 43).
- Tell yourself the storm always passes.
- Use self-kindness on those days that feel overwhelming.
- Create boundaries that are healthy.
- Prioritise what is valuable and important to you.
- Take breaks and reach out for help from those around you.
- Give yourself permission to rest when you need it.
- Talk to a health professional.

Go kindly. Be open and honest about how you are feeling, and don't be afraid to ask for help.

Q&A

WITH SEXOLOGIST **SUSIE TUCKWELL**

Susie Tuckwell is a mother and a highly experienced sex and relationship therapist.

I had an episiotomy and/or vaginal birth trauma. Now I am feeling concerned and anxious about having sex postpartum. How I can work with these feelings?

It is important to allow your body time to heal from any post-birth pain or trauma. Take your time and make sure you are ready. Talk to your partner to foster mutual trust and understanding between each other. You can explore intimacy with yourself first if you are having doubts about how it might feel post-birth. Take sex slow and gentle to begin with, and keep communication open with your partner. 'Outercourse' (such as touching, kissing and mutual masturbation) is often more enjoyable at this stage, and allows the body to get used to arousal and lubrication.

Since becoming a mum I have some insecurities around sex after giving birth such as the changes in my body, breastfeeding (i.e. leaking breasts), low libido, tiredness and fatigue. Are there some things I can do to feel more confident in the bedroom?

Firstly, ask yourself: Who is judging you? Don't be ashamed. Your body has done an amazing thing to not only grow and nourish a human being, but that you are able to feed and care for your baby. There is a small amount of time that your focus will be on your baby and not necessarily your sex life – that is okay.

I often feel overwhelmed by parenthood and not being able to flick the switch from being a mother to a lover. How do I forget the 'mum' jobs and have some spontaneity in my sex life?

It isn't uncommon to feel this way from time to time, particularly in those early months of motherhood. Not many people have a lively sex life – or any sex life at all – soon after a baby. Make sure your partner knows you are feeling overwhelmed and ask for help. It's possible that you are trying to do everything and be everything to everyone. 'Good enough' really is enough: forget perfect. Give yourself permission to spend time with your partner in any intimate way that feels comfortable to you. As time goes on, you will find a balance that is right for you and your partner and for igniting spontaneity in your own way for your relationship. Continue to communicate your feelings to your partner, so you are both on the same page.

As a couple, we are struggling to find the time to have sex – particularly in these early days of having a new baby and the sleep deprivation that comes with that. How can we manage this together?

Many parents feel the same. Sex may not be at the forefront of your mind at this time and that is okay. Over time, you will feel the desire and find the time for intimacy in your relationship. Sexual interest in your partner is more likely if you both work on your love and friendship. Make time for each other, stay connected, ask 'How are you doing?' and be interested in each other's answers. And prioritise sleep, not the dishes, so you are more rested.

Touched out is the notion of having enough of being touched, especially by your baby or children.

Being touched so often and depended on physically, whether cradling, rocking, cuddling or feeding, and having your little one on you round the clock can sometimes be a bit too much.

This is usually experienced by the mother but fathers can also experience it.

Let joy be your focus for the day.

Staying connected

Parenthood can be all-consuming and at times we can let our connectedness to those around us fall to the wayside. This means we can lose touch with our partners, family or friends, perhaps when we need their support the most.

Staying connected is a really great way of taking care of yourself. It can help your emotional health and reduce anxiety and depression, as well as improving your immune system. Connecting with people you love will give you a sense of belonging, which can be especially important during this phase of your life.

You've probably heard the saying 'It takes a village to raise a child'. Your own village may be your parents, grandparents and extended family members, or it could be your close friends, and perhaps new friends from prenatal or mums' groups (see page 184). It can be comforting having that sense of security and support from others, knowing you have people you can call on should you need to. While many of us now live far from our families, there are ways to promote a village network with friends. Here are some ideas:

- **Arrange babysitting swaps for date nights, doctors' appointments, haircuts, etc.**
- **Share exercise time: take turns looking after the babies while the other parent swims or goes for a jog around the park.**
- **Batch-cook meals and swap portions with other families. Or get together for a dedicated cooking day – you'll end up with a full freezer, plus it can be a lot more fun than cooking solo.**
- **Help out with older children to allow each other one-on-one time with your baby: offer play dates, sleepovers, pickups for school and return the favour.**

MUMS' GROUPS

Joining a mums' group, playgroup or mums and bubs class such as yoga, swimming or music can be a great opportunity to meet other parents in your community. The shared experience of having babies of a similar age who are going through the developmental leaps around the same time can reassure you that what you are experiencing is normal. The first year of parenthood can be challenging and you may feel pressure to have your baby reach certain milestones quickly. Offloading concerns, bouncing around ideas and simply chatting with others can be an important part of your social self-care. Because of your shared experience, the mums you meet in pre- and postnatal groups can become some of your closest friends.

Be unapologetically you.

Friendships

When you need support, a kind word or a good laugh, reach out to a trusted friend. This connection can turn your day around and reassure you that you are not alone.

The early days of parenthood can often feel isolating, as we tend to spend more time at home. It can seem easier to withdraw at this time – and if you want to focus solely on this special family time, that is of course completely fine. However, it can be beneficial to connect with your friends – to have a laugh or a cry, or simply enjoy a conversation with another adult! Let your friends know if you want some help – it's likely that they'd love to lend a hand – and consider reaching out to friends with older children when times get tough. They can reassure you that this moment will pass.

Personally, I felt very isolated in those early days; I soon realised I needed to form a village because it is always harder doing it alone. I reached out to friends and began to ask for help when I needed it, which meant I could reciprocate the help and support when they needed it too.

Friendships can change after having kids. As we grow into our new role, we often form new habits and beliefs, and our mindset changes. Our relationship with ourself evolves, and so too does our relationship with the people around us.

Your friends may or may not become parents around the same time as you. We are all on our own path and sometimes we veer in another direction. While it can occasionally be challenging to navigate these different directions, stay open to connection and be honest about how you are feeling.

Staying connected with friends

- Be open and honest. Let friends know if you need to take a pause from attending catch-ups and events. Tell them if you've been feeling lonely.

- Catch up via a videocall or a phonecall if you're unable to meet face-to-face. This is also great when the kids are sick!

- Book in a digital 'sip and paint' evening. Pour yourself a glass of your favourite drink and have fun creating your own artwork, all while catching up with friends.

- Go for a bushwalk or a swim together. Nature, exercise and friendship are a winning combination for self-care.

Social media

Social media can make you feel more connected when you may be feeling isolated or awake at unsocial hours. But it can also lead to unhelpful (and unreal) comparisons with others. Make sure your online engagement serves you well at this time.

Social media platforms can be a valuable resource for many parents, particularly in making them feel less alone and more supported. It is also a great way to link with other families who are going through similar experiences, for example, if you are raising a child with specific needs or parenting twins. You may find a community online that is not otherwise available to you. But be aware that the opinions on social media can also be overwhelming. It is important to take people's experiences as simply that: their experience. Online forums for health-related issues should not take the place of advice from a professional. It can also be easy to become too reliant on followers and likes, or to regard them as a replacement for meaningful connected relationships with those closest to you.

The pandemic really highlighted the importance of taking a break from all media, including news media. Overconsumption can be incredibly stressful and destructive, taking a toll on our thinking patterns and mental health. Taking a break, or limiting what you read, can be good for your health. Find balance between the real and online worlds, and make sure your engagement with social media is working for you.

Take a moment

Answer these questions truthfully and consider how your use of social media makes you feel at this time.

- How do you consume social media?

- What social media do you engage in and for how long each day?

- How do you feel after spending time on social media apps?

- How much are you sharing?

- Are you comparing yourself to others when you use social media?

- How do you feel when you log off or take a break from social media?

We are all **different**.
Our **parenting** styles
are different, our
children are **unique**.
Try not to
compare yourself
to other mums
on the 'gram;
after all, it's just their
highlight reel.

How to make social media more positive for you

- Curate your social media and be selective with what you see.
- Choose hashtags that are positive and that interest you.
- Follow 'real' people who you feel you can relate to.
- Put limits on when you scroll. This may be limiting it in the mornings and the evenings.
- Disconnect when you need to. If you need a break, do it guilt free.
- Consider muting accounts that negatively affect your mental health.

Curate what you read.

Work

The transition back to work after having your baby can be unsettling, no matter how ready you are to return. Talk to your employer about your needs and, if possible, ease yourself back in gently.

It is important to know your rights at work. Become familiar with your company's policy and the relevant laws in your state and country, including flexible work arrangements, leave pay and entitlements and breastfeeding in the workplace.

You may experience guilt or anxiety about leaving your child to return to work. You may be nervous about resuming your professional life. Be aware that this may make you feel more vulnerable than usual. Allow yourself to settle in gradually. Speak kindly to yourself and make sure you set time aside for self-care.

Consider how you can incorporate self-care into your working day. It may be that you can use the commute to exercise, by walking or cycling to work. You may even be able to take a yoga class at lunchtime, or just enjoy a hot cup of coffee for the first time in a long time! Everyone's situation is different, of course, and this may not be possible for you. If this is the case, talk to your partner about how you can maintain your self-care rituals at home and continue to make it a priority.

Finally, know that both you and your child will settle into this new routine. Be proud of who you are and how far you have come.

How to ease your transition back to work

- Be upfront and honest with your employer and discuss your needs and concerns before your return.

- Have a few trial runs at childcare/day care a week or more prior to commencing work. This can make the transition smoother and also allows your baby to settle into a routine.

- Ask for help when you need it. This may include asking to work from home so you can breast pump or feed your baby, reducing your workload, job sharing, or having a private space to breast pump in your workplace.

- Prioritise your mental health and check in with yourself regularly on how you are feeling emotionally.

- Always make time for self-care, no matter how busy you are.

Be proud of
the person and the
mother
you are.
Be proud
of the choices
you make,
the way you
love your family
and raise your
children.

Missives from mums

I asked my community of mums – new mums, mums with young babies, mums with two, three, four children – what they do for self-care. Here are some of the responses I received:

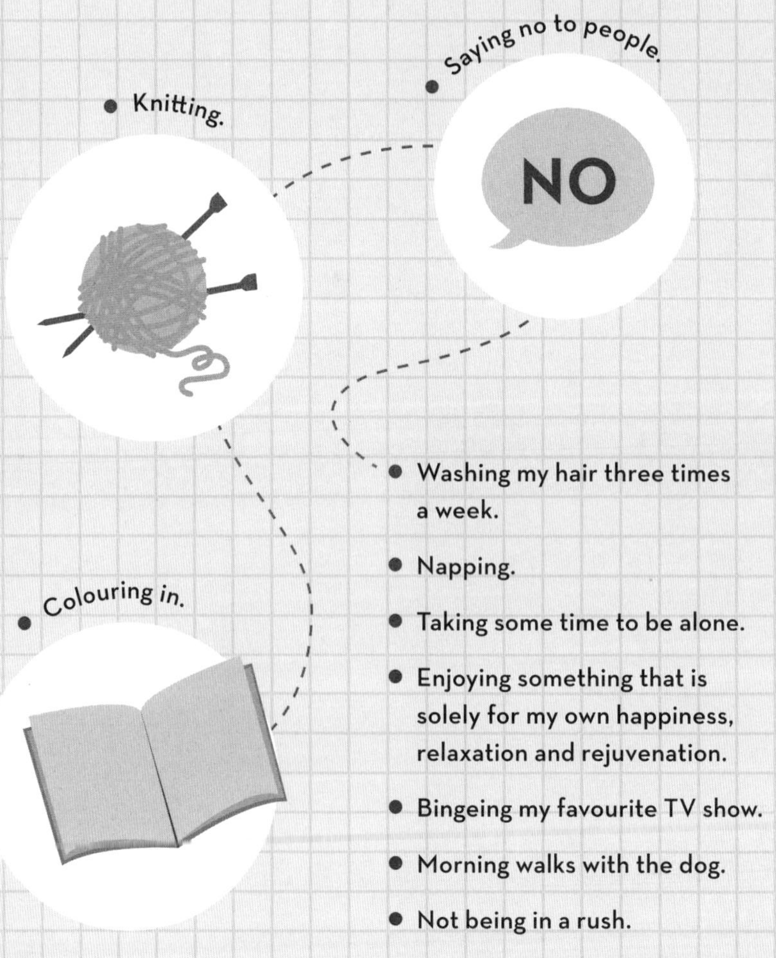

- Washing my hair three times a week.
- Napping.
- Taking some time to be alone.
- Enjoying something that is solely for my own happiness, relaxation and rejuvenation.
- Bingeing my favourite TV show.
- Morning walks with the dog.
- Not being in a rush.

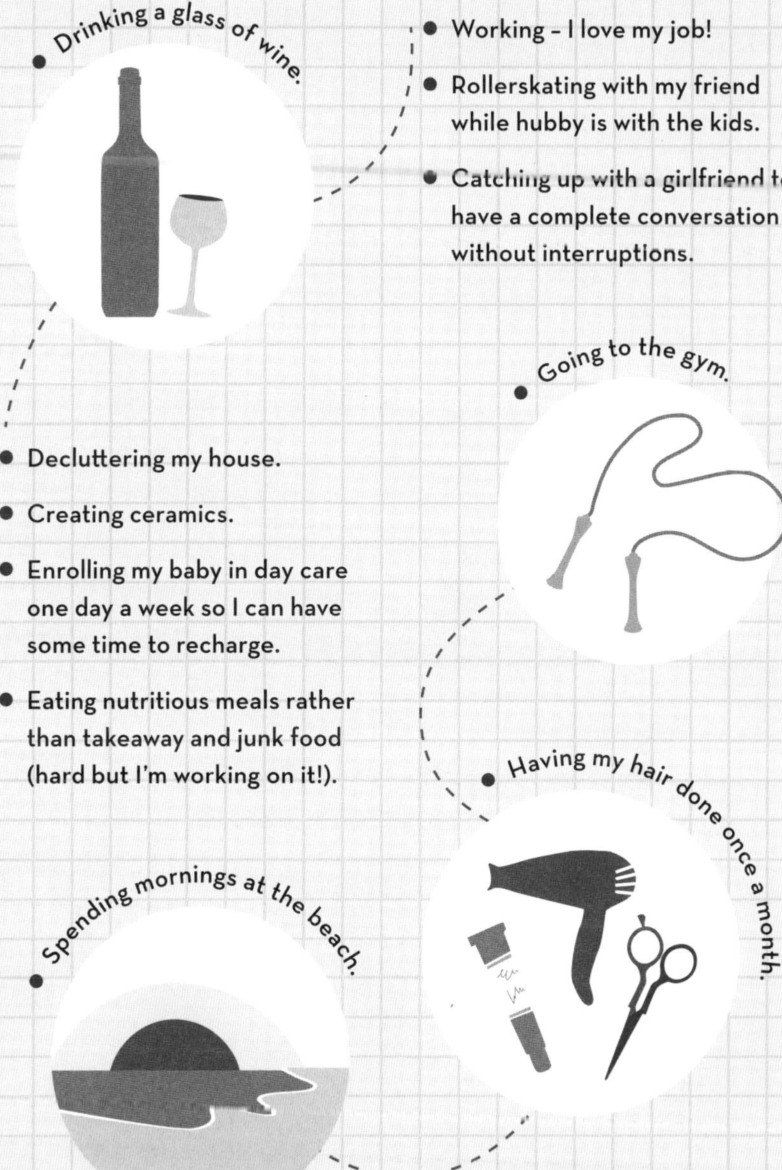
Drinking a glass of wine.
Working – I love my job!
Rollerskating with my friend while hubby is with the kids.
Catching up with a girlfriend to have a complete conversation without interruptions.
Going to the gym.
Decluttering my house.
Creating ceramics.
Enrolling my baby in day care one day a week so I can have some time to recharge.
Eating nutritious meals rather than takeaway and junk food (hard but I'm working on it!).
Having my hair done once a month.
Spending mornings at the beach.

Resources

Australasian Birth Trauma Association
birthtrauma.org.au

Beyond Blue
1300 22 4636
beyondblue.org.au

Helpline available 24/7.

COPE
1300 740 398
cope.org.au

Perinatal support for new parents and parents to be.

The Gidget Foundation
1300 851 758
gidgetfoundation.org.au

Help and support for new parents. Helpline available Monday to Friday, 9 am to 5.30 pm AEST.

Gunawirra
gunawirra.org.au

Community-led program supporting Aboriginal and Torres Strait Islander people, families and children.

Health Direct
1800 022 222
healthdirect.gov.au

Karitane
1300 227 464
karitane.com.au

Parenting services and support.

Lifeline
13 11 14
lifeline.org.au

Helpline available 24/7.

Maggie Dent
maggiedent.com

Parenting help and advice from the Parental as Anything podcaster.

PANDA
1300 726 306
panda.org.au

National Perinatal Anxiety and Depression Helpline available Monday to Friday, 9 am to 7.30 pm AEST.

Raising Children
raisingchildren.net.au

Parenting website with advice for all stages, from pregnancy through to teens.

SMS4dads
sms4dads.com.au

Help and support for dads and dads-to-be.

Tresillian
1300 272 736
tresillian.org.au

Parenting website with advice for all stages, from pregnancy through to teens.

Contributors

Caitlin Dunsford is a mother and physiotherapist with a special interest and further training in the area of women's health. She is incredibly passionate about pelvic health and runs the The Pelvic Floor Project: thepelvicfloorproject.com; @pelvicfloorwithcaitlin

Dr Sarah Hughes is a mother, clinical psychologist and author. She is best known for her work with teenage girls, women's mental health and practical parenting advice. Sarah regularly appears on television, radio and in print media: drsarahhughes.com; @drsarahhughes

Rebecca Ray is a mother, a clinical psychologist, author and speaker: Hello Rebecca Ray, The Podcast; rebeccaray.com.au; @drrebeccaray

Meagan Rose is a mother of two and a registered dietician who is passionate about postnatal nutrition and health. Meagan has worked in Sydney and Newcastle, NSW.

Susie Tuckwell is a mother, grandmother and highly qualified sex and relationship therapist in Sydney, NSW. Her therapy approach is based on research and supports clients with a wide range of sex, relationship and communication issues: susietuckwell.com.au

Acknowledgements

I'd like to acknowledge the Traditional Owners of the land on which I live and write. I pay my respects to Elders past and present and am mindful that this land always was and always will be Aboriginal Land.

A huge thank you to the wonderful team at Pan Macmillan. I am so grateful for all the support, guidance and help you've given me. A special thank you to Ingrid Ohlsson, Ariane Durkin, Naomi van Groll, Libby Turner and Emily O'Neill.

Thank you to my beautiful family: my husband Ben, my two babies, my parents and my brothers for their unwavering love and support.

Index

F

G

H

I

J

K

L

M

N

O

P

R

S

T

U

V

W

Y

Pan Macmillan acknowledges the Traditional Custodians of Country throughout Australia and their connections to lands, waters and communities. We pay our respect to Elders past and present and extend that respect to all Aboriginal and Torres Strait Islander peoples today. We honour more than sixty thousand years of storytelling, art and culture.

First published 2022 in Macmillan
by Pan Macmillan Australia Pty Limited
Level 25, 1 Market Street, Sydney, New South Wales
Australia 2000

A catalogue record for this book is available from the National Library of Australia

Design by Emily O'Neill
Edited by Libby Turner and Megan Johnston
Index by Helena Holmgren
Colour + reproduction by Splitting Image Colour Studio
Printed in China by 1010 Printing International Limited

10 9 8 7 6 5 4 3 2 1